The
Great Way
of all beings

Paul Ferrini

Book Design
by Paul Ferrini and Lisa Carta

Cover art: Li Po by Liang K'ai
(begining of the 13th century)
Tokyo National Museum

Library of Congress Catalog Card Number: 00-106792
ISBN 1-879159-46-5

Manufactured in the United States of America

HEARTWAYS
PRESS

P.O. Box 99
Greenfield, MA 01302

Renderings of Lao Tzu

Table of Contents

to the masters of Tao

One who dies

and is not forgotten

lives forever

Introduction

The Great Way of All Beings: Renderings of Lao Tzu is composed of two different versions of Lao Tzu's masterful scripture *Tao Te Ching*. Part one, *River of Light,* is an intuitive, spontaneous rendering of the material that captures the spirit of the *Tao Te Ching*, but does not presume to be a close translation. Part Two is a more conservative translation of the *Tao Te Ching* that attempts as much as possible to stay with the words and images used in the original text.

Part One uses the metaphor of the river to convey the Taoist emphasis on spontaneity and surrender to the flow of life as it unfolds. In Part Two, however, a different water metaphor arises. It is not the river moving with confidence toward the sea, but water flowing inward, forming a quiet lake surrounded by pine trees, or a pond gleaming in the moonlight. It is water moving toward stillness, toward the gateway of "the mysterious female."

The words and images used in Part One are more contemporary. They leap out from the center to explore how the wisdom of the Tao touches us today. By contrast, the words and images of Part Two turn inward toward the center, offering a more feminine, receptive version of the material.

Anyone familiar with the Taoist tradition knows that the creative and the receptive balance each other and male and female complete each other. A number of people have asked me which of the two versions contained in this book I prefer. How can you say you prefer the creative to the receptive, the spontaneous to the restrained, or the mind of "sudden understanding" to the mind of "awareness steeping"?

You, dear reader, may choose whichever one you like. As for me, my favorite seems to be "whichever one I'm reading at the time."

Namaste,

Paul Ferrini

PART ONE

River
of Light

A word about "Renderings"

Lao Tzu was my first teacher. Coming out of an Atheist upbringing, I could not find God in the churches and synagogues of the west. Nor was I drawn to the elaborate rituals of Hinduism, the sparse monasticism of Theravadin Buddhism or the heady metaphysics of Mahayana Buddhism.

I was drawn instead to the wide open spaces of nature and to the poet who understood them. Taoism to me was never a religion, but a state of consciousness and a way of life. Lao Tzu was my teacher from the moment I read the words "The way that can be spoken is not the true way."

He was my teacher, because he rejected all outward authority. The God of this teaching was not to be found in scriptures or rituals, but in the hills and streams and in the tidewaters of the heart.

River of Light is the Tao that is written by my teacher's footsteps along the streambeds where we have walked together. It is not an attempt to translate the words that have been attributed to him, so much as an attempt to elucidate the awareness that I have always felt singing to me through those words.

11

This is my poem to his poem, and his poem to the poetry of my being that lives with him always. There are realms of mercy and forgetfulness here I cannot describe to you. We have been drunk together, looking up at the stars. We have crossed the river by moonlight. Together, we have found the boat that only comes at dawn.

The waters that have carried us are moving in these pages. Now the boat belongs to you. May it take you into the heart of his teaching.

Namaste,

Paul Ferrini

River
of Light

Truth cannot be conveyed in words

Truth cannot be conveyed in words.
Words disguise the subtle essence.

We give names to truth,
but these names are as unreliable
as a finger pointing at the moon.

As soon as the moon rises,
the finger points to empty skies.

Let's face it.
Truth is naked, unadorned.
It has no name. It has no form.

Nameless and formless,
the subtle essence gives birth
to all the forms that walk the earth.

Words and concepts come later,
giving rise to all kinds of theories,
explanations and beliefs.

Complexities abound.
Misunderstandings proliferate.

The more words people use,
the harder it is to understand them.

❮❯

Truth is not to be found in thinking
or conversing.

It is not to be found in preferences
or opinions.

If you want to find the subtle essence,
get quiet and accept what is.

❮❯

Wise beings do not engage
in selective seeing.

They see what is in front of them,
whether it pleases them or not.

To see what is, is to rest in the Tao.
Tao is neither for nor against.

It has no expectations.
It makes no judgments.

It is transparent like a window.
It lets in both sunlight and shadow.

Thinking you know

Thinking you know is the beginning of darkness.
Knowing that you don't know is the beginning of light.

These are not two, but one and the same.
Herein lies the mystery.

Knowing is based on comparison

Knowing is based on comparison.
One thing seems beautiful
only because something else seems ugly.
Good seems good
only because something else seems evil.

Without poverty, there would be no riches.
Without difficulties, nothing would be easy.

Without long, there would be no short.
Without silence, there would be no sound.

All the opposites arise
in relationship to each another.

⌒

The wise one understands
that front and back follow each other.

That is why she is happy to move back
and let others go ahead of her.

Even when a fool offers to lead the way,
she happily stands aside.

Not interfering with the flow of life,
she goes where the river takes her.

When others wear out,
she takes the lead.

Because she is aligned
with the current of the river,

she has phenomenal strength
and endurance.

While she cannot restrain her creativity
or withhold her love,

She does not overpower
or control others.

When people do not respond,
she moves away.

Ever playful, she allows life
to unfold spontaneously.

Pull the boat up on the beach

Preferring one person over another
creates jealousy.
Desiring what you do not have
creates discontent.

So love the person in front of you.
Do not wonder why s/he
does not fit your pictures.
Throw away your pictures.
Empty your mind.
Do not waste your time
contemplating the ten virtues.
Grab the rope
and pull the boat up
onto the beach.

When each person is as s/he is,
there are loaves and fishes enough
to go around.

When nobody wants to be
like someone else,
Tao shines like a golden sun
in the hearts
of women and men.

Expect nothing

Tao is a perfect vessel.
It contains all there is.
The more wine you pour,
the more remains.

Some come expecting miracles,
yet the real miracle
is to expect nothing.
When you expect nothing,
everything can be given
to you.

The universe has no preferences

The universe has no preferences.
It uses whatever is available.

Thus, actions of great significance occur
without thought or deliberation.

Life is simple, but people make it difficult.
They can't stop judging and having opinions.

Debating the scriptures,
they forget to breathe.

Deaf to the drumbeat in their hearts,
they discuss "the nature of reality."

Thus the pathway to the infinite
is forsaken.

The more words you use,
the more confused people become.

Fools speculate on "original cause."
Those who know aren't talking.

The spirit of the valley

Mist rises to the mountaintop,
yet without the valley,
there would be no mountain or mist.

The spirit of the valley never dies.
It is the Great Mother.

Both the ignorant and the wise
suckle at her breast.

She is the soil that surrounds the root,
the embrace that holds the river
in its banks.

Forget the Mother
and the root withers and dies.

Rest in the Mother
and the veil that separates the two worlds
opens wide.

The Friend is not afraid of intimacy

Some people are afraid of intimacy.

They cannot surrender to you
for fear of losing themselves.

But the friend is not afraid.
He gives himself to you with abandon.

No matter how much he likes you,
he knows he cannot lose himself.

The friend has tattered clothes,
yet does not hesitate to give you his coat.

His shoes are torn and muddy,
yet he gladly kneels to wash your feet.

Supporting others on their journey,
he moves forward on his own.

He knows that helping others never hurts,
and holding others back never helps.

Watch him carefully. He stays back,
yet finds himself at the head of the line.

He is content to sit alone,
yet people surround him.

He desires nothing,
yet every one of his needs is met.

Tao is like water

Tao is like water.
It occupies all the hidden places.
It is gentle, yet penetrating.
There is no nook or cranny
beyond its reach.

Tao teaches us to be gentle
with others. It teaches us to give
without thought of return;
then people are not afraid
to invite us into their hearts.

Tao helps us learn
to be flexible about little things,
yet firm in our purpose.
It shows us how to navigate
around the needs of others,

as water moves
around trees and rocks.
Tao is like water.
It lulls people to sleep.
It wins their trust.

No one is afraid of water,
yet when its power
is released,
no dam can hold it back;
no riverbank can contain it.

The river is gentle and sustaining,
yet it cannot be moved off-course.
No matter how many obstacles
lie in its path, it always
finds its way to the sea.

Sharpen the knife; fill the cup

Over-sharpen the knife
and even a tiny mistake loses your finger.

Keep counting your coins
and a thief will see you.

Take the credit
and you'll get the blame.

Why keep working
When the work is done?

To fill the cup,
stop short of the brim.

When body and spirit unite

When body and spirit unite,
there is wholeness.
Relaxed, yet alert, you have
the playful awareness

of a child.
What you know in your heart
and what you see with your eyes
are not at odds.

Because you love the people,
you can lead without deceiving them.
You greet them with open arms
as a mother greets her child.

You make no speeches,
demand no tributes,
yet the gates of heaven
open and close at your feet.

Like the great Mother,
you nourish without possessing,
serve without taking credit,
lead without raising your flag.

Whole in yourself,
gentle with others,
Tao flowers
in your heart.

Something and nothing

Without space inside the rim,
the wheel is too heavy;
without spokes,
the wheel has no strength.

Without clay,
the cup cannot be formed;
without the space inside,
it can't function as a cup.

You can't have a room
without walls,
but what good are walls
without windows and doors?

Something is useless
without nothing.
Nothing has no purpose
without something.

The eye is blinded by what it sees

The eye is blinded by what it sees.
The ear is deafened by what it hears.
The palate is tainted by what it tastes.
Thoughts drive the thinker mad.
Money manipulates the maker.

Therefore the wise see without looking,
hear without listening,
taste without eating,
understand without thinking
and make money without trying.

Not defined by others

Praise props you up;
criticism casts you down.

Both come from the outside.
Both are temporary.

Be wary of favor or disfavor,
grace or disgrace.

Be that which is not defined
by the opinions of others.

The desire for name and fame will control you.
Be happy being nobody.

Misfortune comes to those
who take themselves too seriously.

Have a good laugh at yourself.
That's the best medicine for arrogance and pride.

Because you hide your light,
people take pleasure in finding it.

Thinking you are harmless,
they follow you.

They have no idea
that you are taking them home.

Tao says wake up

You look right at it,
but you cannot see it.

Your ear is on its belly,
but you do not hear it.

You are touching the drum
but have no idea that it is being played.

Like a sleepwalker you move through life
unaware of where you are going.

Tao says wake up.
Tao says open your ears and your eyes.

Tao says feel the vibration of the primordial sound,
which has no end or beginning.

Tao says "This is it. Pay attention, you dummy!"
But you go on sleepwalking.

Imagine what would happen if Tao too
went to sleep.

Where would the sleepwalker be?
In what world would the drum sound?

The Masters walk in the hills

Even today the masters walk in the hills and valleys
where you live.

When you greet them they smile at you,
but remain silent.

Crossing the river on a warm winter's day,
they step on the stones

where the ice has melted
and the water splashes cool and luminous.

Visiting you, they bring simple gifts,
yet never overstay their welcome.

When the village is buzzing with turmoil,
they sit profoundly still.

When the village sleeps, they carry on
strange conversations

with the moonlight on the river.
Follow them and you see

order within chaos
and exceptions to the rule.

Look about you, friends.
When you know the answer

before the problem arises,
you know they are in your midst.

Truth needs an empty mind

Food needs an empty stomach.
Truth needs an empty mind.

For something new to come in,
something old must be released.

Mourn your losses; bury the past.
From rituals of closure, the die is cast.

Stop *doing* and *being* is born.
Self is revealed when masks are torn.

Some say the Emperor has no clothes,
but the truth is he has more than you.

Until you have the courage to disrobe,
others cannot see who you are.

The cannon

From the deepest stillness,
activity arises.
From Oneness, the ten thousand things
are stirred into being
and run their course.

When their creative energy is expended,
they fall back to their Source.

Tao is the cannon
hidden behind each display of fireworks
exploding in the sky.
It is pure potential, recycling the old
and harnessing the new.

Do not become lost in the changing pattern.
Fall back to the changeless.

Return to the engine of being.
Take root in the Source of all manifest things.
Do not be the firecracker going off
or the gunpowder ignited.
Be the cannon.

True and false leaders

True leaders are one with truth.
They inspire us, but take no credit.
Therefore they are invisible.

Next are those who tell the truth.
We rarely hear what they have to say.
They are infrequently quoted
on the evening news.

Then come those who stretch the truth
or twist it in support of their agendas.
We gladly give them
our money and our votes.

Finally, there are the pathological liars.
They are so convincing,
it never occurs to us that they
want anything other than to serve us.

We naively place the well-being
of our families, our businesses,
and our country in their hands.

When the great Tao is forgotten

When the great Tao is forgotten,
people dedicate themselves to serving God.

When serving God becomes inconvenient,
people build churches
and throw a few coins to the poor.

Morality replaces the direct experience of the divine.
The cleverness of the mind is valued above
the surrender of the heart.

⌇

When the great Tao is forgotten,
temples are built and priests are ordained.

When common sense is forgotten,
universities spring up offering advanced degrees.

When the love in the family disappears,
people talk about "family values."

When the country betrays its original vision,
leaders make patriotic speeches.

Those who seek love

Give up outer knowing
and discover the wisdom that comes
from within.

Give up the commandment to love
and appreciate people
as they are.

Give up duty and rediscover kindness.
Give up riches and poverty
will end.

Keep your life plain and simple
and you will stay close
to your true nature.

Don't waste your energy yearning
for what you do not have.
Be joyful right now.

Those who seek love only push it away.
If you want love to find you,
leave it alone.

My mother is without form

Others are entertaining and bright.
I am slow and dull.

Others go to the park and climb the terraces.
I walk aimlessly by the river.

Others claim what's right and protest injustice.
I do not know what justice is.

Like a newborn babe before it greets its mother,
I am unschooled in the ways of the world.

My mother is without form.
Her breast rises and falls under me

like the waves of the sea.
Others resist the wind or fill their sails.

I have no preferences.
I have no direction.

I do not know where I have been.
I do not know where I am going.

The form in which truth appears

Truth comes from the Tao.

It is unpredictable, elusive.
The form that expresses truth today
may not express it tomorrow.

When form no longer expresses truth,
Tao withdraws its support
and the form collapses.

Tao presides over the birth
and death of forms.
It destroys, creates, embodies.

Because of this, you cannot point at the form
and say "This is true,"
nor can you say "this is not true."

While Tao is constant,
the form in which truth appears
is constantly changing.

Yield and you move ahead

Yield to others and you move ahead.
Bend a little and the way becomes straight.

Empty yourself and be filled to the brim.
Work like an ox, sleep like a baby.

The less you take, the more you gain.
The more you relax, the longer you hold the pose.

Thus, the wise person does not call attention to himself,
yet people constantly seek him out.

He pretends to be ordinary,
yet others praise and celebrate him.

Because he does not seek recognition,
it comes to him of itself.

Because he is humble and unassuming,
people are not jealous of him.

They are happy for him
when good fortune comes his way.

Therefore, the ancient wisdom tells us,
"yield and you will go forth.

Simply be yourself and all that you need
will come to you."

Trusting the Tao

To talk a little is natural.
To talk a lot is unnatural.

A gentle rain is best for the crops,
yet even the hardest rain comes to an end.

Only humans make storms that last for days.
Only humans chatter away in the dark.

The hardest thing for us to do
is to trust the Tao.

Not recognizing the hand that stirs the sauce,
we stir with a vengeance

and the sauce flies out of the bowl.

Our canvas is assaulted by overturned jars
of carefully held paint.

Our ears ring from the orchestrated din
of accidents waiting to happen.

The Tao waits on us, but we refuse to order.
We won't eat dinner

till our own goose gets cooked.

Some things are obscene

Some things are obscene:
tall people on stilts;
fast people on steroids;
rich people robbing the poor.

If you think you are great,
and proclaim it from the rooftop;
don't be surprised
if pigeon shit falls on your head.

It is easy to take more than you need.
It is easy to say more than is necessary.
That's why Taoists live modestly
and say only what needs to be said.

We have no other name for it

Born of the mystery
before heaven and earth came to be:
silent, empty, centered in itself,

yet constantly giving birth;
it is the Mother of the ten thousand things.

It has no name. It has no face.
We call it Tao,
because we have no other name for it.

We say it is the still point of the turning wheel,
because we have no other concept for it.

Flowing outward from its center,
it moves to the furthest edges of the universe
and then returns to itself.

Tao is full of wonder.
Heaven and earth are wonderful too.

The wise being who knows these energies
is also filled with wonder.

The path of the human is to follow the earth.
The path of the earth is to follow heaven.
The path of heaven is to follow the Tao.

Tao rests in itself.
Without moving, it goes everywhere.

She carries the Tao in her heart

As movement comes from rest,
so the branches of the tree
grow from its roots.

Traveling to foreign countries,
the woman of Tao feels at home.

Strangers are like members
of her family.

Thrilled by vistas
of sea and sky,
she remembers the pear tree
in her garden.

Even when there is commotion
around her,
she seems relaxed and at ease.

That's because she carries the Tao
in her heart.

If those who have do not share

Walk lightly and you leave no tracks.
Speak with heart and people understand you.
If you have common sense and fairness,
you don't have to keep adding things up.

A good door opens and closes.
A good binding comes on and off.

The great one takes care of people
according to their need;
he does not pamper people,
nor does he abandon anyone.

This is the action of wisdom
and compassion.

What is a fulfilled man
except a teacher of an unfulfilled one?
What is a rich man,
but a redeemer of a poor one?

If those who have do not share
with those who do not have,
the Tao is not honored,
and confusion and resentment grow.

No matter how many words you say to the contrary,
this is the crux of the mystery.

A skilled tailor

A skilled tailor cuts only where he has to.
Actions are only the tip of the iceberg.

Therefore act like the male,
but rest in the female.

What good are mountain and sky
without the embrace of water?

Yes, know the heights,
but remain in the valleys.

Know your worth,
but stay humble.

The Taoist is refined,
yet he seems simple and unaffected.

He is highly individuated,
yet you cannot spot him in a crowd.

When something needs to be done
he knows exactly what to do.

Yet when no exigencies arise,
he seems as dense as a block of wood.

Like a skilled tailor, he relies on his eyes
more than his scissors.

Not-fixing

As soon as you think something needs to be fixed,
you forsake the Tao.

The universe is sacred exactly as it is.
It cannot be improved.

Only a fool tries to fix something
that isn't broken.

Though human beings
try to impose their own rules on nature,

they inevitably fail.
Nature takes direction from no one.

Whether coming or going, behind or ahead,
strong or weak, leading or following,

the wise are not taken in.
Understanding the nature of change,

they avoid extremes,
and appreciate people as they are.

Not fighting

Do not advise others to fight,
for fighting is not the way of Tao.

Briars grow where armies have passed;
heartache and sorrow are never far behind.

In those rare situations where force is timely,
it is economical and swift.

There is little, if any, loss of life.
One achieves results

without puffing oneself up
or humiliating others.

No amount of force can win the people's love.
If you want to rule, put your weapons away.

Kindness and restraint
get the attention of the people.

War has one outcome

War has one outcome only.
Winning or losing is a funeral.

Fools use weapons
at the least provocation.
They delight in killing
and rejoice in victory.

Intelligent people use weapons
only when there is no choice.
They regret savagery
and take no pleasure in victory.

Followers of the Tao
do not use weapons;
they know that to do so
is to admit defeat.

They use their knowledge
and intuition to diffuse conflict
and bring people
back to their true natures.

The river of tears

Tao is the mightiest force in the universe,
yet it cannot be located.

Without it, there would be no galaxies.
Without it, there would be no sub-atomic particles.

Because it is without form,
it cannot be adequately described.

Once the universe expresses as name and form,
Tao becomes hidden.

Don't become lost in the drama.
Know when to stop.

Tao is like the river of blood that feeds your heart.
It is like a river of tears bringing you home.

Mastering the self

To know others is admirable.
To know the self is essential.

Mastering others gives outer power.
Mastering self gives inner power.

The greatest riches are gained
when you know you have enough.

Then, whatever you do bears fruit.
Even when you die,

you are not forgotten, but live on
in the hearts of the people.

Tao goes where it is needed

Tao flows to the left and the right.

Without deliberating, it fulfills its purpose.
It simply goes where it is needed.

Tao supports the ten thousand things,
yet you would never know it.

It keeps the ship from sinking
and brings in the crop,

but the captain and the farmer
take all the credit.

That's okay. Tao needs no thank you.
It prefers to remain obscure.

Because no one expects anything from It,
Its action is miraculous.

Tao cannot be exhausted

In the end, all things return
to the Tao.

Strangers think they are attracted
to the free music and food,

but we know the Tao
has no taste or sound.

While it cannot be perceived
by the senses,

its usefulness cannot
be exhausted.

No matter how much you drink,
the cup is still full.

Deep waters

It is natural for the hard to become soft,
and the strong to become weak.

Push it and it stumbles.
Squeeze it and it crumbles.

Aim hard and throw a wild pitch.
Raise it to the rafters and it falls in a ditch.

Put your jewels on display
and your house will be robbed.

Be wise and keep your resources hidden.

The only fish that are caught
are the ones that leave deep waters.

Stillness and Peace

We say that "Tao does this" or "Tao does that,"
but the truth is Tao does nothing.

It simply holds the space of perfection
and nothing is left undone.

If our leaders knew how to hold this space,
peace would come to the land.

Rules would no longer be necessary,
for the inherent order would prevail.

When things rest in their center,
there is no wanting or seeking.

When there is no wanting or seeking,
there is a profound stillness and peace.

Waiting for the fruit

The wise person smells the flower,
but waits for the fruit.

He knows that a good person
doesn't always look good.

The wise person pays more attention
to actions than to words.

He knows that those who talk a lot,
accomplish little,

and those who make speeches about justice
have their own agenda.

People inevitably rebel
against the empty promises of their leaders.

Then, martial law is declared,
and tanks roll through the streets.

The wise leader knows you cannot compel
the people's trust.

That is why he dwells on what is real.
His ear is to the hearts of the people.

Wholeness/Integrity

Things live in their wholeness.
They thrive in their integrity.

Sky is high and overarching.
Earth is firm and understanding.

Spirit is trusting and playful.
It animates the ten thousand things.

If sky were not expansive, it would fall down on us.
If earth were not solid, we would sink into it.

If spirit could not move, it would not enliven
and the ten thousand things would shrivel and die.

Each thing is asked only to be itself.
Being itself, it is neither humble nor proud.

It simply performs its purpose.
Let our leaders take note.

They are not here to be all things to all people.
They are here to be themselves.

Returning to their origin

Tao originates and concludes in Oneness.

The ten thousand things begin as one thing,
and expand by dividing.

When individuation no longer serves their growth,
they learn to yield, merge, simplify,
and so return to their origin.

Tao abides with you always

Oneness exists prior to being and not being.

The clever pretend to understand this,
but it really baffles them.

Average minds give this no thought.
Halfwits laugh as if they have been told a great joke.

If it were not for this laughter,
Tao would not be Tao.

That is why we say "The more light, the darker the path.
The easier the footing, the more you go astray."

Great purity lies in a gutter.
Great virtue always finds contempt.

The greatest truths cannot be spoken.
The highest notes cannot be heard.

Yet, do not despair.
That which is without name or form

is as close to you as your next breath.
Tao abides with you always.

No matter how many mistakes you make,
It brings you to fulfillment.

The causes of violence

A violent person dies
a violent death.
Consider then
the causes of violence
within yourself.

Each one
of the ten thousand things
carries within itself
the seeds of conflict
and reconciliation.

Every coin has two sides.
Black comes with white,
male with female,
rich with poor,
yin with yang.

First you meet the enemy
and you run. When
you know there's no escape,
you turn around
and make a friend.

Do not be afraid
to lose yourself
in the arms of another.
You're just learning to love
another part of yourself.

Land is nourished by water

Land is nourished by water,
mountain by clouds and mist.

That which is hard
yields to the soft.

That which is visible
rests in the invisible.

The action of Tao
arises from non-action.

The truth of Tao
originates in silence.

Better to have nothing

What is more important:
to be famous or to be yourself?

What is better: to be rich
or to do the work you love to do?

Which hurts more: profit or loss?

Better to have nothing and enjoy
the richness of this moment.

Life never disappoints
the man or woman of Tao.

That is because s/he never expects it
to be different than it is.

The crooked path

While the erudite give sermons,
those who know are mute.

Sometimes the crooked path
is better than the straight one.

Perfect in its imperfection,
it does not outlive its use.

When Tao is visible

When Tao is visible
horses run wild through the fields.
When Tao is hidden,
wild stallions and mares
are captured and saddled.

It is a great mistake to take
what does not belong to you.
Every animal you steal
you have to water and feed.
Every bag of money you seize

you have to carry.
It does not seem like it at the time,
but the primary casualty
of your greed
is your own freedom.

The wise already know the outcome

Remaining still and centered
you can know all that is worth knowing.

The furthest mountain is as vivid
as the tree outside your window.

The wise already know the outcome
of the journey.

That is why they are not pushing and shoving
to get through the door.

Light through the window

Learning means gathering facts.
But the Taoist knows
he must carry the weight
of every fact he gathers.

Thus, for every fact you give him,
he gives you one back.

If you insist on quoting chapter and verse
from some obscure scripture
or cumbersome
code of law,

be prepared to listen
as he reads the fine print
in your car manual
or life insurance policy.

Taoists do not accumulate
money or knowledge.
Whatever comes into their hands
leaves by them.

Whatever goes into one ear
passes out the other.

The Tao proceeds majestically
by letting things take their course.
Thus, the goal of the Taoist
is to stop interfering with what is.

Each day he surrenders some belief he has
until he has no beliefs left.

Knowing nothing,
he becomes transparent.
Then, instead of blocking the light,
he lets it come streaming through.

Learning to meet the needs of others

I learned to meet my own needs a long time ago.
Now I am learning to meet the needs of others.

Caring for happy people isn't very hard;
they appreciate your efforts.

But try caring for unhappy people
who resent you and treat you unkindly.

Try loving those who do not love you,
or trusting those who do not trust you.

Try having faith in those
who have no faith in you or in themselves.

Yet this is what the Tao asks.

If you don't give love,
people continue to hate.

If you don't give trust,
people continue to be suspicious.

If you don't give faith,
people remain depressed and suicidal.

Unless they receive love,
people cannot learn to give it.

Unless they receive trust,
people cannot learn to trust others.

Unless they receive faith,
people cannot learn to have faith

in others
or in themselves.

Meeting the Challenge of Life

Some people live like they are ready to die.
They complain about what they are missing,

yet turn away from opportunities
that could bring new energy into their lives.

Life is never good enough until death comes.
Then suddenly it passes muster.

Don't take these moments for granted.
Don't wait until death shakes your hand to start living.

The man or woman of Tao knows
this very moment is miraculous.

S/he knows that right now
it is a great privilege to be alive.

That is why s/he does not stay at home
when a rhinoceros or a tiger passes by,

but follows them confidently into the jungle.
When life is passionate and full,

there is no place for death to get a foothold.
Even in danger, under the shadow

of horn and claw, you cannot hide
or withdraw your energy.

You must rise to meet
the challenge life asks of you.

When love is given freely

All things arise from Oneness
and are nurtured by it.

One becomes many.
Formless becomes form.

Tao is the Mother of the ten thousand things.
She is loved and honored by all her children.

This is the nature of things.
No one holds a gun to the child's head.

No one legislates gratitude.
When love is freely given, it is a virtue.

When it is expected or demanded,
it is a ball and chain.

Virtue grows in the hearts of women and men.
It is nourished, cared for, sheltered and protected.

Thus, it guides without controlling
works without taking credit,

leads without dominating,
loves without possessing,

and gives without fear
of being used up.

Bizarre behavior

When the behavior of the sons and daughters
seems bizarre,

return to the Mother.
Then you will be safe from harm.

Keep silent.
Stop feeding your desires.
Stop running around in circles
thinking you are important.

Until you have the strength to put your cell phone down,
you are beyond hope.

Insight means seeing the subtle ways
you avoid contact with yourself.

Tend to your garden

Why stray from the trail
when it is well maintained and has the best views?

People are always looking for a better way
than the one they are on.

That's why there are so many detours
and cul de sacs.

Tend to your garden
and the family stays fed.

Work with others to irrigate the crops
and the village prospers.

With prosperous villages, the district thrives
and the country experiences abundance.

But all this prosperity comes to an end
when your garden is full of weeds.

As soon as you take something you haven't earned
by the sweat of your brow,

the balance of giving and receiving
is thrown off.

When you have more money than you need,
you invent all kinds of uses for it.

You buy fancy clothes.
You wear expensive jewels.

You indulge yourself with food and drink.
You buy boats, airplanes,

and build summer houses
on the mountain or at the beach.

Meanwhile, farmers cannot get a loan
to plant their fields,

and granaries remain empty.
You think you are beyond danger's reach,

but it is not true. Hungry people will soon
be knocking at your door.

All this selfishness is obscene.
It is not the way of Tao.

Cultivating virtue

What is well planted is not easily uprooted.
What is held tightly cannot slip away.

If you establish true virtue in yourself,
others cannot threaten it.

If you cultivate true virtue in your family,
your children cannot be led astray.

If virtue is nurtured in your actions
toward your neighbor, he will not betray you.

If virtue is internalized in the hearts of people,
nations will not be drawn into wars.

The virtuous one

The virtuous one is protected.
Scorpions and vipers do not sting him.
Lions and tigers do not chase him.
Birds of prey do not circle over his head.

Women are powerfully drawn to him
yet he will not touch them.
Although virile and self-confident,
he is not provocative or flirtatious.

Men seek to draw him into their affairs,
but he has no interest in them.
His mind cannot be tempted.
His loyalty cannot be bought.

Others gather for sport or ceremony,
but these events do not satisfy
his spiritual hunger. He prefers
to walk alone by the stream.

Some spiritual seekers rush about
in a buzz of activity.
They meditate, pray,
and try to control their breath.

This appears virtuous,
but it is really a waste of energy.
It gives people work to do,
but it does not enlighten them.

The virtuous one knows that
incessant activity is not the way of Tao.
He does not worship an external God,
so he does not need elaborate costumes

or rituals. He does not seek
an internal God so he does not need
complex breathing
or meditation techniques.

He is content to be himself,
to abide with what is, to enjoy
the simple, amazing beauty
that surrounds him in each moment.

Dim your brightness

Those who know don't talk much.
Those who don't know can't seem to stop talking.

It isn't hard to spot a fool,
but you have to go out of your way
to find a wise woman or man.

Keep your mouth closed
and you won't invite misunderstanding.
Learn to soften when you feel anger rising.

Do not flaunt your intelligence.
Do not be arrogant or proud.
Dim your brightness so others may speak.

Pull the dark shroud of peace around you.
Be one with the dust that rises.
This is your fate in the end.

Better get used to it.
Once you have come to this station,
You don't care if the train comes or goes.

What is the difference
between good and bad, love and hate,
honor and disgrace?

Today your friends help you;
tomorrow they deceive you.

Today your enemies attack;
tomorrow they help you bury your dead.

Not controlling people

If you want to govern,
you must show fairness and restraint.

Be constant, but not too predictable.
Refrain from making restrictions and laws.

The more you try to regulate the lives of people,
the more out-of-control things become.

Do not encourage violence
by flaunting your army or your weapons.

Let your soldiers feed the homeless.
Let your ministers care for the elderly and the sick.

The virtuous leader loves his people
but does not try to reform them.

Although he makes no sermons about the costs of crime,
lying, cheating, and stealing diminish.

Although he does nothing to improve the economy,
wages go up steadily and new businesses thrive.

Refusing to take credit, he avoids the limelight,
yet people love him and praise him.

Following his example, they learn to simplify their lives
and take pleasure in small things.

Rule with a light hand

Rule the country with a light hand
and people will be innocent and playful.

Rule with an iron first
and people will be cunning and deceitful.

Happiness cannot be found
if you are afraid of suffering.

Order cannot be discovered
if you are overwhelmed by chaos.

Meet life where it is
and integrity will be preserved.

Be slow to judge
and you won't be bewitched.

The wise one is sharp, but he does not offend.
He is one-pointed, but he does not prick.

He is clear and determined,
but not arrogant or overpowering.

He illuminates the darkness
without showing his light.

Restraint/Moderation

Shallow roots cannot withstand
sudden gusts of wind.

The deeper the roots,
the stronger the branch.

Restraint is the ruler's paintbrush.
Take it away and he cannot paint.

If you have not learned moderation yet,
learn it now.

Then, you can pick up all the paint
you have splattered

in impulsiveness and haste,
and start with a clean canvas.

Of all the virtues,
this one is the greatest.

Even the great mother had to show restraint
when giving birth to the ten thousand things.

Too much fussing

Ruling the country is like cooking a small fish.
Too much fussing destroys it.

Those who understand Tao pay evil no mind.
It's not that they are stupid or lack vigilance.

They simply know that problems
follow those who look for them,

and evil has no power to compromise anyone
who is firmly established in the Tao.

Mother prepares the ground

The river occupies the lowest place
yet is fed by streams from the highest mountains.

The female attracts the male by lying still
and letting him come to her.

A thriving country expands its wealth
by keeping its borders open to trade.

It is not necessary to be aggressive
to gain great influence.

If you want to expand, you must learn to yield.
If you want to give, you must learn to receive.

The Creative accomplishes wonderful things,
but only because the Mother prepares the ground.

The gifts of Heaven are great
but they must be brought down to earth.

This is the Mother's doing.
The Father may inspire and uplift,

but all things that are truly helpful in this world
are the Mother's doing.

All things tend toward Tao

All things tend toward Tao.

The virtuous set their compass for it,
and those who stray from the path
find their way back in the end.

You do not give up on a stray dog.
Why abandon a man or woman
who loses the way?

Flattery can buy attention.
Good deeds can buy respect,
but none of these come from the heart.

If you want to gain the leader's friendship,
do not send horses and jade.
Send him a few words of truth.

If others sin, offer them forgiveness.
Then, your own mistakes
will not condemn you.

The Tao is magnificent.
Those who seek it, find it.
Those who avoid it, also find it.

Many small deeds

Work with joy in your heart
and something of consequence will get done.

Sip the soup and you can taste it.
Swallow it and the taste is gone.

Give profound attention to the smallest things.
Simplify the complicated.

Great acts are made up of many small deeds.
Be patient and industrious

and the hardest tasks will be accomplished
without great struggle.

Make big promises and others will be disappointed.
Take things lightly and difficulties will come.

Thus, the wise one lets things take their course,
and confronts each challenge as it arises.

It seems as if she is doing nothing special,
yet under her watchful eyes

works of great beauty
are brought into being.

Nip trouble in the bud

Nip trouble in the bud,
and peace extends itself easily.

Care for things when they are small
and they grow strong.

The towering oak tree
starts as a fragile sapling.

The nine-storied garden
begins as a row of flowers.

If you want to traverse the globe,
you must take the first step.

Go to sleep and the fox sneaks in

When people have success,
it often goes to their heads.

They get sloppy in their actions.

They go to sleep at their watch
and the fox sneaks in.

Reacting too slowly,
they overcompensate.

Thus, a small mistake
becomes a big one.

The wise one brings people back
from their errors.

He helps them become free of desires
that hold them back.

He helps them find forgiveness
for their mistakes.

He leads them back to their true nature.

Not teaching

In the beginning,
the wise ones did not teach Tao,
so Tao could not be misused
or misunderstood.

Not aware that they were
missing anything,
people were content
to live simple lives.

Once Tao was taught,
teachers were lifted onto pedestals.
Worldly concepts were passed off
as spiritual truths.

Outright lies and deceptions
were accepted as canon law.
Teachers got lazy and fat.
Their students became greedy.

Church and state
became a single engine,
taking people's money
without remorse or apology.

This happened many years ago,
but it is not much different today.
Even if you search diligently
on every city street

and every forest path,
you will be lucky if you can find
a single man or woman
who understands the Tao.

Seek the lowest place

Water does not seek to rise above,
but to dwell underneath.

That is why it can nurture the land.

If you want to serve the people,
you must be humble.

Listen to those who have not been heard.
Attend to those who have been neglected.

Like water, you must seek the lowest place.

Be gentle and determined,
and you will reach your goal.

Let those who are angry
pass you by.

Let those who are impatient
go in front of you.

Do not compete with others.
Just move ahead at your own pace.

That way you will arrive without injury,
passing those who stumbled

or tired themselves out.
Remember, the turtle beats the hare.

Because he is not in a hurry,
he eventually wins the race.

Three treasures

There are three treasures
you must find and keep.

The first is compassion.
The second is simplicity.
The third is humility.

From compassion comes courage.
From simplicity comes abundance.
From humility comes leadership.

Today, people try to be brave
without feeling compassion for others.

They try to be generous
without first saving their money.

They try to lead the way
without learning what people need.

All this leads to disaster.

Rather, be compassionate
and truth will be served.

Live a simple, honest life
and people will support your cause.

Follow in the footsteps of others,
and you will learn to lead them.

Not abusing one's position

The best soldier is calm.
He does not lose his temper.
He is not easily provoked.

The best winner is gracious.
He does not brag about his victory
or put his opponent down.

The best employer is empowering.
He corrects without shaming people
or dwelling on their mistakes.

Because he does not abuse
his position, he keeps it.
This is the way of Tao.

Winning the war without weapons

A wise soldier would rather take a step back
than one ahead.

This is called marching in place,
or rolling up your sleeves without showing your skin.

The wise general attacks when the enemy sleeps.
She wins victory without taking a single life.

Because she never underestimates her opponent,
she is never caught off-guard.

Her mind is so clear
that some say she could go to war

without any weapons
and win.

The jewel of understanding

My words are easy to understand
and practice,

yet people are baffled and confused.

They do better with a teaching
that tells them what to do.

That is why I walk alone in the forest.

Only a few bother to follow,
but even they cannot find me.

Those who take my name in vain
are honored as pontiffs and kings.

That is the way the world is.

That is why the wise person wears simple clothes,
eats what is offered to him,

and disappears for long periods of time
into the mountains.

The jewel of understanding
cannot be given to fools.

It must be held quietly
in the heart.

True Wisdom

To know that you do not know is true wisdom.

Thinking that you know when you don't
is the major obstacle to realizing the truth.

Therefore, surrender your concepts.
Throw away your beliefs.

Rest in that state of not knowing
where everything is a mystery.

When humans lose their sense of awe

When human beings lose their sense of awe,
trouble abounds.

Heaven and earth separate.
The skies darken. The ground trembles.

Hostile people become bloodthirsty.
Gentle people become fierce.

Therefore, take care.
Do not invite strangers into your home.

Do not gossip with people at work.
Keep to yourself

and to those you know you can trust.
These are dangerous times.

The net of Tao extends far and wide

A passionate person will kill or be killed.
A compassionate person will survive.

Those who are restless and impatient
come to a quick end,

while those who are patient stay alive.
Heaven does not favor impulsiveness.

Tao does not strive, yet it overcomes.
It does not speak, yet its purpose is known.

People do not beseech or pray to it,
yet it arrives in the nick of time.

The net of Tao extends far and wide.
Its fibers are rough; it has been sewn

and mended countless times,
yet it works as well as it did when it was new.

It keeps pretense out.
Falsehood cannot slip through.

The master executioner

Tao gives and takes away.
Even the sage does not understand how or why.

Yet humans decide they will be judge and jury.
They put people to death for petty crimes.

But instead of frightening the criminals,
this makes them more determined.

Humans forget there is a master executioner.
Trying to take his place is sheer madness.

A master carpenter cuts straight without a rule,
while a novice has difficulty following a pencil line.

Not only does the novice build a crooked house;
if he is careless, he loses a finger or a hand.

A crust of bread

When their bellies are empty,
people will start a civil war
over a crust of bread.

Why are people hungry?
Because government taxes
take food off their tables.

Why are people rebellious?
Because the laws of the land
interfere too much in their lives.

Why aren't people afraid to die?
Because no one gives them
a good reason to live.

Meek and gentle inherit the earth

Babies come into this world gentle and weak.
Old people leave this world rigid and tough.

Roses grow to be full and soft.
Then they wither and die.

Stiff and unyielding is the language of death.
Flexible and yielding is the language of life.

An army that's too harsh feeds upon itself.
A tree that will not bend is broken in the wind.

Hard and merciless fall in the end.
Meek and gentle inherit the earth.

Stringing the bow is an art

To string the bow, you must stretch it.

If you do not stretch it sufficiently,
the string will be too slack,
and the arrow will not fly far from the bow.

If you over-stretch the bow,
the string will be too taut,
and it will be hard for you to pull it back.

Stringing the bow is an art.
The archer must learn how to do it
before he aims his first arrow.

Leadership is also an art.
It takes from those who have too much,
and gives to those who do not have enough.

This is the way of heaven.
Yet today's leaders get it all mixed up.
They take from the poor and give to the rich.

They overwork the weak and rest the strong.
Instead of righting the balance,
they over-tip the scales.

If it weren't for the inherent stability
of the Tao,
such mayhem would never cease.

They are not afraid of the people's pain

Nothing is more gentle or yielding than water,
yet it can wear down the largest stones.

In nature, the weak overcomes the strong,
and the flexible outlasts the rigid.

The man and woman of Tao remain invisible
until disaster strikes.

Then they appear where they are needed
and work without ceasing.

They are not afraid of the people's pain.
They do not react to the people's fear.

Because they act with certainty,
people follow their lead,

risking their lives
to save the lives of others.

Without them, the country could not be rebuilt,
yet they refuse to take credit.

When the sick have been healed
and the dead have been buried,

they disappear into the forest
or onto the mountain path.

Not forcing others

Resentment often lingers
when agreements are broken.

Thus, the wise person does
as she promised she would do,

and trusts her opponent to do the same.
Even if her opponent

makes only a half-hearted effort,
she does not get angry or complain.

She knows that all she can do
is play her part.

Even the Tao
cannot force others to do something

they are unable
or unwilling to do.

Walking in the forest is his greatest joy

The Taoist prefers to live
where there aren't many people.

He prefers the mountain hut
to the village square,

the small town to the big city.
The Taoist prefers to keep things simple.

Though machines are available,
he does not use them.

He would rather walk,
than ride in a carriage.

He would rather swim,
than ride in a boat.

Though many fine weapons have
been given to him by leaders,

he has no use for them
and doesn't even display them.

He knows how to write,
but prefers to tally by knotting a rope.

His food is plain,
his clothes coarse and simple.

Since he has nothing people want,
he doesn't lock his door.

He waves to his neighbors,
but he doesn't visit them.

Though he hears the crowing of cocks
and the barking of dogs

in the next village,
he rarely goes there.

He finds great joy walking in the forest
or sitting quietly by the river.

His wisdom deepens
as he grows older.

When he can no longer
get out of his bed,

he surrenders his body to the Tao
and dies in peace.

Giving the credit to others

Words that are true
are not always beautiful.

Words that are beautiful
are not always true.

A wise person
does not waste her time arguing.

She does not moralize
or quote the scriptures.

She does not waste her energy
accumulating riches,

but gives her resources
to those who need them.

Because she gives without sacrifice
resources continually come to her.

She is tenacious,
but would not hurt an ant or a fly.

Heaven blesses her work,
but she remains humble

and gives the credit to others.

Postscript: Song of the River

The action of water is steady.

It bears down continually,
yet it is never in the same place.

That is the mystery.

When the river moves
it catches the light.

It has the spontaneity of this moment,
yet time is on its side.

It cuts a channel thousands of feet deep
inside the mountain.

Way down, you can see
the surging green waters,

running over the rocks,
and you can hear the song

of the white waters.
Follow the twisting path

down to the riverbank.
Listen carefully and notice

how, amid the roar of falling water,
everything becomes still.

PART TWO

Tao Te Ching

The Unchanging Truth

A word about this translation

After completing *River of Light,* I walked into a bookstore and was greeted by a new translation of the *Tao Te Ching* by Richard John Lynn (Columbia University Press, 1999). This literal English translation of the Chinese original, along with the introduction and commentaries by Wang Bi (who lived about 200 years after Lao Tzu), provided me with exactly the kind of scholarly work I needed to consider making a closer translation of the *Tao Te Ching.* So I decided to do another version of the material.

This second version invited me to be with the *Tao Te Ching* in a different way. Instead of using it as a springboard to explore new ground, I found myself drawn into its mysteries. Before writing, I immersed myself in the literal translation and commentaries like tea leaves steeping in hot water. After all, the tea had to brew before it could be served. The result, I hope, makes for a good cup of tea, retaining the flavor of the original, even when it reaches beyond it.

Paul Ferrini

1

The unchanging truth
cannot be expressed in words.
That which is eternal and constant
cannot be given a name.

The truth has neither name nor form,

Naming it, we call it Mother,
because it gives birth to us,
nurtures us, and sustains us,
but it is not our Mother.

This is the mystery.

Caught in the web of desire
you see the ten thousand things.
Resting in the heart,
you see their subtle origin.

Manifest and unmanifest,
named and nameless,
are different but arise
from the same Source.

This is the mystery of all mysteries.

2

You cannot have beauty
without ugliness,
or good without evil.

Absence and presence,
difficult and easy
describe each other.

Long and short,
high and low
measure each other.

Musical notes
depend on each other
for harmony.

Therefore the sage
allows things to be
as they are.

He acts without deliberation
and teaches
without using words.

He shows people
how to tend to their gardens,
but leaves the reaping to them.

He gives
without needing to control,
loves without

needing to possess.
helps without needing
to be appreciated.

Thus, he remains
in people's hearts
forever.

3

If you praise one person too much,
others will be envious.

If you value certain goods too much,
they will soon be in short supply.

If you don't want people to be greedy,
stop telling them what they are missing.

Fill their bellies
and their minds will be free of desires.

Strengthen their bones
and the intensity of their cravings will diminish.

When people do not seek abstract knowledge,
or material possessions,

they do not become restless
or dissatisfied.

Not feeling impoverished within,
or coveting what others have,

they feel free to be themselves
and get along easily with others.

4

Tao is like a limitless black hole.

It is so wide you cannot find the edge of it.
It is so deep you cannot find the bottom of it.

Universes spill out from it.
Others swim in its depths.

Try to pierce it and it swallows your knife.
Try to bind it together and it unravels.

It is so bright, you cannot see its brilliance.

It is so humble, you can stand on it
without knowing it's supporting you.

5

Heaven and earth do not try to be good.
Their action is impersonal,
arbitrary, and unpremeditated.

The sage also acts without reference
to any moral code.
She obeys her inner nature.
Her actions are spontaneous
and unrehearsed.

The space between heaven and earth
is like a great organ.
When the wind blows, the pipes sound.
When there is no wind,
the pipes remain empty
and make no sound.

The sage knows
that many words are tiresome.
Like the empty pipes of an organ,
she waits in silence
until the wind stirs.

6

The spirit of the valley never dies.
Without her, the myriad creatures could not exist.

All beings nurse at her breast
yet her milk is never exhausted.

Although she is formless,
she sustains those who have taken form.

That is why she is called
"the mysterious female."

That is why her gate is called
"the root" of heaven and earth.

7

Heaven and earth are eternal.
That is because they do not exist for themselves.

The sage acts in harmony with heaven and earth.

Because he lets others go ahead of him,
people notice him.

Because he makes no effort to sustain himself,
he is fed and housed like a king.

Because he is not selfish or fussy about his needs,
he feels fulfilled in each moment.

8

The highest good is like water.

Because it seeks the lowest places,
It can nourish the myriad things.

Tao is like that.
It feeds the roots, not the branches.

If you want to live in harmony with Tao,
build your house close to the ground.

Let your thoughts stay close to silence.
Be kind to others and truthful in what you say.

Be disciplined within, even-handed without.
When acting, be still and wait for the right time.

Do not contend with others
and no blame will come your way.

9

When you pour too much in,
the cup overflows.

When you over-sharpen the blade,
the knife breaks.

Too much gold and jade
attract thieves to the hall.

Name and fame are destroyed
by arrogance and pride.

The secret of an abundant life
is knowing when is enough.

10

Can you rest in your essence
where the only true safety lies?

Can you trust as a baby trusts
and be gentle and undefended with others?

Can you see with your heart,
not just with your eyes?

Can you understand people
without analyzing them?

Can you be yourself
without eclipsing others?

The true leader softens his light
so that others may shine.

He supports people
without trying to control them.

He mentors people, yet allows them
to make their own mistakes.

The true leader empowers others.
He does not call attention to himself.

Indeed, he makes himself seem dense
so his mastery will not be noticed.

11

Thirty spokes unite at the center of the wheel.
Without the empty space between them,
the wheel cannot function.

Mud and water combine to make a clay vessel.
Without the empty space inside,
the vessel is useless.

If you want to make a functional room,
you need to cut holes in the walls
for windows and doors.

Nothing derives its purpose from something.
Something derives its usefulness
from nothing.

12

Don't see only with the eyes
and the five colors will not blind you.

Don't listen only with the ears
and the five sounds will not deafen you.

Don't taste only with the mouth.
and the five flavors will not nauseate you.

When people are distracted
by sensual stimuli,

they veer away from
the natural course of their lives.

They look to others for guidance
when they should be trusting themselves.

That's why the wise feed people's bellies,
not their eyes.

With a full stomach, people's desires
come and go without creating havoc.

13

Favor and disgrace are equally alarming.

Both are based on the opinion of others.
Neither one is based on your inherent worth.

Why make your happiness conditional
on how others see you?

Why let the changing tide of public opinion
dictate your worthiness or lack of it?

Be steady in favor or disgrace.

When success comes, do not cherish it.
When failure comes, do not let it hold you back.

Success is not a reward.
Failure is not a punishment.

No matter what happens, be yourself.

Things unfold according to the Tao.
Do not take them personally.

Those who take things personally
cannot find peace in their own minds.

How can they rule the country?

But those who accept favor and disgrace
with the same equanimity,

those who remain themselves
in hope and in despair,

are fit to have all of heaven and earth
entrusted to their care.

14

You look for it, but you can't see it.
You listen for it, but you can't hear it.
You reach for it, but you can't touch it.

Resting in the original unity,
it is impossible to apprehend.

When it rises, it brings no light.
When it sets, it brings no darkness.

It appears without a purpose.
It disappears without a trace.

Since it has neither name nor shape,
you cannot say that it exists.

Yet since all things depend on it,
you cannot say that it does not exist.

Try to meet it and you cannot find its head.
Try to follow it and you cannot see its tail.

Yet wait patiently and you will know
that the thread of Tao is present now.

Although it has no name or face,
although it has no beginning or end,

it is the same Tao
that people knew in ancient times.

15

The old masters of Tao
were in step with the great mystery.

Their actions were subtle
yet so deeply rooted,
few people understood them.

They walked carefully like a woman
crossing a stream in winter.

They were poised and alert,
like a man surrounded by enemies.

Polite as a guest, yielding
like ice melting in the spring,
they adapted to all circumstances.

Yet they were also solid and inscrutable
like an uncarved block of wood.

Who could describe them?
They were empty like a valley.
They were opaque like murky water.

Yet stir the water and it would become clear.
Interrupt their quietude
and they would shoot into action.

The masters of Tao
were prepared to act, but rarely did.

They preferred to remain ready, alert,
capable, like an unfilled cup.

16

Let your mind be free of thoughts.
Accept your life just as it is.

Notice how all things arise, flourish
and then return to their roots.

When you return to your roots,
you begin to fulfill your destiny.

Fulfilling your destiny,
you become constant and reliable.

Being constant and reliable,
you are inclusive and impartial.

You embrace all things equally.
Thus, you become capable of ruling.

Heaven abides with you.
Tao expresses through you.

For as long as you live,
you dwell in abundance and peace.

17

The greatest leaders are invisible.

Without calling attention to themselves,
they inspire others to accomplish great things.

Next are those who rule like kind parents;
people are fond of them.

Then come those who rule by force;
people fear them.

Finally come those who rule by deception;
people despise them.

Leaders who don't trust the people
do not win the people's trust.

Wise leaders hold the vision
and work hard to manifest it.

When they succeed,
they give the credit to others.

In this way, they earn
the people's undying devotion and love.

18

When the Tao is forgotten,
morality and righteousness appear.

When great books are studied and quoted,
people find ingenious ways to avoid the truth.

When love is lost in our relationships,
kindness and duty appear.

When the country betrays its vision,
flags are waved and people enlist.

19

When you stop seeking enlightenment,
you discover the plain and simple truth.

When you stop preaching morality,
kindness to others is natural and spontaneous.

Stop wearing jewels and expensive clothes
and thieves no longer follow you home.

Stop showing off your beauty and intelligence
and people begin to trust you.

A fool envies another person
because of what s/he has or how s/he looks.

A wise person sees and cultivates
the inner qualities that give rise to success:

clarity of vision, resourcefulness, dedication,
tenacity, trust, and generosity of spirit.

20

The search for knowledge is not peaceful.
Try and separate the rose

from its thorns
and you destroy its beauty.

Seeking approval, you invite criticism.
Seeking praise, you invite disgrace.

Caught in the pursuit of happiness,
people don't see how despair dogs their feet.

They go to the feast and climb the terrace
as if they were going to live forever.

I alone am quiet and indifferent.
I am like an infant before its first smile.

I have no direction or ambition.
My consciousness is like that of a stupid person.

While others are bright and obvious,
I am dim and obscure.

I have lost my capacity to discriminate
between praise or blame, less or more.

I mix everything up.
To me they appear the same.

Floating without care on the great sea,
I have no fear of rising water or wind.

While others row passionately toward shore,
I am content not to steer.

21

Because it anticipates everything,
Tao is said to be empty.
Yet within its emptiness,
some essence abides.

Because you cannot see its origin,
Tao is said to be dark.
Yet within its darkness,
some subtle light hides.

Though on the surface
forms are constantly changing,
the essence in the center
is changeless.

Essence of the changing,
light of the darkness,
something in nothing,
this is the Father.

Though lost in the dark womb
of the Mother,
He is totally authentic
and true to Himself.

Name within the nameless,
form within the formless,
His presence has been felt
since the beginning of time.

Without Him, Mother could not
give birth to the myriad things.
Without Him, there would be
no manifest existence.

22

Stepping aside,
she does not lose an arm or a leg.

Bending down,
the falling branch misses her head.

Working devotedly,
her energy is constantly renewed.

Having just a little,
she stays centered and close to her roots.

She shines
without turning up her light,

makes her point
without insisting she is right.

Neither arrogant nor selfish,
she does not arouse the enmity of others.

By stepping aside,
she keeps her wholeness intact,

and thus becomes
a model for others.

23

After talking for a while,
it is natural to become silent.

The windstorm does not last all morning.
Heavy rains do not fall all day.

Movement and stillness alternate.
Silence and sound follow each other.

Only human beings try to make things last forever.
In so doing, they precipitate change.

Trying to hold onto their riches,
they lose them.

Trying to try to hold onto their successes,
they unexpectedly fail,

Trying to keep their virtue perfect,
their desires take them by surprise.

The Taoist knows
that everything that happens has a purpose.

So when something comes, she accepts it.
When it leaves, she lets it go.

She learn to trust life
and so life does not abuse her.

Even when the winds of change
are whirling around her,

she stays in the center,
in the eye of the hurricane,

where everything is quiet
and completely still.

24

Standing on tip toes — just touch him
and he loses his balance.

Seeking to impress others — just ignore him
and he feels maligned.

Insisting that he is right,
we can't help questioning his motives.

Bragging about his achievements,
his insecurity stands out.

Acting self-important,
we wonder how he can motivate others.

Tao says: too many dishes spoil the feast.
Vanity destroys the man.

25

The ten thousand things
arise and pass away,
but there is something
that does not arise
and does not pass away.

All forms are subject
to change,
but there is something
without form
that does not change.

Indivisible and whole
in itself, it existed
before heaven and earth.
We call it Tao,
but it has no name.

We refer to it as
"the gateway of the mystery"
because all things arise from it
in the beginning
and return to it in the end.

Four things are great:
Tao is great;
heaven is great;
earth is great;
the leader is great.

The leader follows the way
of earth. Earth follows
the way of heaven.
Heaven follows
the way of Tao.

Tao follows nothing.
It is the way of all things.

26

That which is heavy sinks to the bottom.
It is the root and the foundation of the light.

Non-action is the root of fortuitous action.
Silence is the foundation of honest speech.

When the leader travels he stays well hidden.
Although master of many chariots,

he travels lightly. Beauty surrounds him,
but he does not stop to admire it.

Although invited to many social functions,
he prefers keeping to himself.

Even when interacting with others,
he stays centered within.

Since he does not lose himself in the world,
he remains capable of governing it.

27

There are no tracks where she walks.
There are no whispers when she speaks.
She does not have to keep a tally
to know where things stand.

Although she has no lock, no one
can open what she has closed up.
Although she has no rope, no one
can untie what she has bound together.

Neither rewarding nor punishing,
she does not raise one person up
at the expense of another,
but inspires each according to his ability.

Thus, no one's genius is discounted.
No one's contribution is denied.
She sees light in others and they light up.
Even criminals become gentle and loving.

Because she is so humble,
people forget how important she is.
Yet when she leaves even for a single day
order and peace are lost in the village.

People engage in all kinds of disputes.
Without her presence to remind them,
people forget who they are
and cannot find their way back home.

28

The Taoist is capable of great acts,
yet he restrains himself.

He lies in wait like the great Mother.
He withdraws into himself
like a river valley.

Although he is infinitely wise,
he appears as innocent as a baby.
Even when he is treated badly,
he remains undefiled.

Knowing that glory and disgrace
come hand in hand,
he suffers each with equanimity.

Others fall apart when tested in this way.
They resort to all sorts of means and plans.
They resist what happens,
and so they do not learn to master it.

The Taoist remains as steady and patient
as a block of wood.

Even when he is given the knife,
he refuses to cut.
He knows the suffering of the people
will diminish by itself.

Because he understands wholeness,
he knows the cloth is best
when it is left uncut.

29

The laws of heaven and earth
are immutable.

Why try to change them?
Why take a horse and try
to make it behave like a pig?

The universe is sacred.
If you try to improve it,
you will destroy it.

If you try to control it,
you will lose control
of your own life.

For some it is natural to lead;
others prefer to follow.

Some breathe through the nose;
others through the mouth.
Some are strong; others weak.

Some are restless; others lazy.
The sage allows all people
to be as they are.

Thus, he eliminates confusion.
When people have no desire
to be like others,

it is easy for them
to fulfill themselves.

30

The Taoist leader does not use force
to gain control over others.

He does not covet the land of others.
He has no new taxes he wants to impose.
He prefers to allow things to remain
in their inherent integrity and order.

He knows that where armies have gathered,
weeds and brambles grow,
and the year after a military campaign
is a year of famine and hardship.

A wise leader defends the state
by outsmarting the enemy.

Although he could easily attack and win,
he allows the vanquished troops
to surrender
and withdraw in peace.

He does not need to draw blood
to make his point.

He achieves victory,
but does not brag about it.
He asserts himself when necessary,
but doesn't step over the line.

He knows that one trespass
leads to another,
and those who live by the sword
eventually die by it.

31

Weapons are instruments of disaster.
In the end, they hurt the people.
Thus, the Taoist avoids them.

The virtuous leader uses weapons
only when there seems to be no choice.
Thus, he is sad even in victory.

To take delight in killing people
no matter how cruelly they have acted,
is against the way of heaven.

When the battle claims many lives,
the leader arrives with a heavy heart.
He makes no victory speeches.

He does not vilify his enemies.
He joins with friend and foe alike,
mourning the dead on both sides.

32

The great leader is like a block of wood
that has not yet been carved.

He does not cherish opinions.
He does not make up his mind
until the facts are gathered.

Not influenced by what others think,
nor swayed by his own desires,
he acts authentically
and with fairness to others.

Emulating him,
people trust their inner nature
and treat others with respect.

Thus, they live in harmony.

But when the leader acts
for personal gain or to impress others,
competition and strife arise
in the hearts of people.

That is why a great leader
looks carefully at his own motives.

Even when he acts forcefully,
he is vigilant for signs
that it is time to stop.

Thus, danger is avoided.

The great leader knows
that all actions must return
to their roots in stillness
to remain centered in the Tao.

What goes out must come back in.
What goes up must come back down.

It is the nature of the tides
to ebb and flow.

It is the nature of mountain streams
to flow down into rivers,
and for rivers to flow down
into the sea.

33

One who knows others is wise.
One who knows herself is wiser.

One who prevails over others is strong.
One who prevails over self
is stronger still.

One who has money is rich.
One who is contented is richer still.

One who acts diligently is successful.
One who acts skillfully
is more successful.

One who makes few mistakes
holds her place.
One who learns from her mistakes
is promoted.

One who lives a good life dies in peace.
One who lives a life of Tao
lives forever
in the hearts and minds
of the people.

34

The Tao is like a great river with many tributaries.
It stretches out in all directions.

Tao sustains people without their knowing it.

It gives them food, clothing and shelter
without asking for anything in return.

Because it asks little, people think of it as small,
but without it people would not achieve fulfillment.

The ten thousand things arise from it
and return to it in the end, but forgetting their origin,
how could they know their destination?

The action of Tao is gentle and continuous
like waves lapping the sand.

It acts consistently without effort,
never attempting to do more than it can.

Although barely noticed,
it accomplishes extraordinary things.

35

Tao is without form,
yet all of us turn to it
to find peace and safety.

Music and food entertain us,
but Tao eludes us.

We look for it,
but it is hardly visible.

We listen for it,
but it is scarcely audible.

We taste it,
but it has barely any flavor.

All of us rely on the Tao,
but none of us can find it.

Because we can't perceive it
with our senses,
we think it does not exist.

36

If you want to weaken a person,
let him grow strong.

Let him flourish, expand,
and grow overconfident.

Do not oppose him
or endeavor to restrain him.

Let him go and he will trip
over his own feet.

The understanding of the Taoist
is both subtle and deep.

He knows that only gentleness
overcomes brute strength;

only those who bend at the waist
are not broken in half.

Without revealing his strategy
he is gentle and polite,

patient and accommodating.
He knows that to keep the fish,

you must dangle the bait,
without showing the hook.

37

Tao acts without deliberation,
yet everything of value is accomplished.

If our leaders could act in this way,
peace on earth would be established.

When desires arise,
the Taoist lets them come and go.

She does not indulge them,
nor does she seek to control them.

She just lets them be.
Thus, they have no impact on her.

When desires have no impact,
all things return to their natural state.

38

Only pretenders to virtue
strive to be virtuous,
good, kind or holy.

One does not seek "virtue"
until the Tao is lost.

One does not desire "goodness"
until he knows that virtue
is beyond his reach.

One doesn't embrace "kindness"
until he knows that
goodness may pass him by.

One does not strive to be "right"
until he abandons kindness.

Virtue arises spontaneously.
It requires no thought or action.

Goodness arises compassionately.
It requires simple thoughts
and loving actions.

Kindness arises deliberately,
with careful thoughts
and considerate deeds.

Righteousness arises predictably
with moral thoughts
and obedient deeds.

The wise leader sees in righteousness
the beginning of disorder.

He is not content to hide behind
moral absolutes or spiritual pride.

He looks for substance at the root.

When the tree blooms,
people offer him the flower,
but he prefers to wait for the fruit.

39

All things refer back to the One
and are sustained by It.

Thus, heaven is pure.
Earth is stable.
Gods are worshiped.
Valleys are filled.

Sustained by the One,
life forms naturally prosper,
and leaders naturally
provide constancy.

Can you imagine a time
when heaven is weak,
earth unsteady,
and gods no longer speak?

Can you envision a time
when valleys are dry,
entire species die,
and cultures fall apart?

This is what happens
when the One is forgotten.

Thus, all that is high up
finds its foundation in the lowly.
All that is lofty and proud
finds its roots in humility.

The greatest leader
never puffs himself up.
To him the greatest praise
is no praise.

He prefers being a stone
hidden in the depths
of the river
to a shining piece of jade.

40

Becoming soft and flexible,
we return to our roots.

This is the action of Tao,
which embraces
and gives life to all things.

Yet the roots of Tao
are not in form.

When it returns to its roots,
it becomes invisible
and indescribable.

41

When the wise one hears the Tao,
he practices it diligently.

When the intelligent one hears the Tao,
he retains some of it and forgets the rest.
When the slow one hears the Tao,
he lets out a belly-laugh.

If he did not laugh at the Tao,
it would not be Tao.

Tao seems to be in front of you,
but when you reach for it,
it eludes your grasp.

It seems to be elegant
and smooth like silk,
but when you wear its robe,
it is as rough and shapeless
as a burlap sack.

Its light is so humble, it seems dark.
Its purity is so unassuming,
it seems impure.
Its virtue is so indiscriminate,
it seems unvirtuous.

Its square regulates our affairs
yet it has no corners.
Its vessel carries us forward
yet it has no sides.

We listen for it,
yet its note can't be heard.
We look intently for it,
yet its image can't be seen.

Although it has no beginning,
it leads us back
to our original nature.

Although it has no end,
it helps us come to completion.

42

After Tao gives birth to a single manifest one,
that one quickly becomes two,
and two becomes three.

This is how the myriad things come into existence,
one after another. There is no end
to the proliferation of names and forms.

To follow the Tao, you must learn to simplify.
You must return from the many
to the original one.

How is this done? Listen carefully.
To return to the one, stop puffing yourself up,
stop striving, stop seeking more.

Take what you have and give some away.
Simplify. Reduce. Give over. Give up.
When your belly is empty,

take only what you need to live.
Stop being a man or woman of importance.
Let your reputation fall in the muck.

Diminish your consumption.
Curb your appetites and desires.
Give up your opinions and preferences.

Accept yin equally with yang,
understand their interdependence
and the energetic processes they share,

and you will return to the original manifest one.
Between that one and the Tao,
there is an immense chasm.

Crossing it is like moving between something
and nothing, between being
and non-being, between life and death.

While others may teach about this,
I leave it alone.
Words cannot describe it.

Images cannot represent it.
Each one will understand how to cross
when s/he gets there.

43

Air enters earth from above.
Water enters earth from below.

That which is yielding and flexible
penetrates that which is hard and fixed.

Thus, non-being penetrates being.
Unanticipated events penetrate well laid plans.

Acting without conscious intent,
delighting in surprises and epiphanies,

patient and accommodating
when obstacles arise,

not-forcing and not-striving,
the Taoist reaches his goal gracefully.

He lives life without effort.
His teaching is conveyed without words.

44

Which is more important: who you are
or who others think you are?

Which is more important:
what you do for a living
or how much money you make?

Which causes greater harm:
having too little or having too much?

Step on others on your climb to the top
and they'll plot to drag you down.

Refuse to share your riches with others,
and you'll be a target
for parasites and thieves.

Content to be yourself, you won't
be disturbed by what others think.

Gentle with others,
you won't provoke their anger.

Not accumulating
more than you need,
people won't covet your resources.

Living simply and unobtrusively,
you will avoid danger
and live a long and happy life.

45

Things are complete
when you allow them
to be incomplete.

They are full
when you allow them
to be empty.

They are straight
when you allow them
to be crooked.

They are skillful
when you allow them
to be clumsy.

They are eloquent
when you allow them
to be silent.

They are abundant
when you allow them
to be simple.

They are moving
when you allow them
to be still.

46

When the Tao prevails
we are content to stay at home.
We use horses to till our fields
and shovel manure
to fertilize our gardens.

When Tao ceases to prevail,
horses are bred for war.

When the supply
of warhorses becomes scarce,
mares in foal are saddled up
and colts are born
on the battlefield.

Nothing causes more hardship
than lack of contentment.
Nothing causes more suffering
than craving for
what one does not have.

47

Without leaving your house,
you can know all of heaven.
Without looking out your window,
you can see Tao at work.

If you try to know Tao
from its manifestations,
you will just get confused.
In seeking the many,
you will lose the one.

If you want to understand Tao,
stay where you are.
Take no deliberate action,
but remain at the root.

Once you embrace the one,
the ten thousand things
will reveal their secrets to you.
You will not have to
seek them in the world.

48

On the path of learning,
more information is needed.
On the path of Tao,
less information is needed.

Having less information,
you have less to do.
Having less to do,
you rely less on your own action.

Relying less on your action,
you allow things to be
accomplished without planning
or deliberation.

Thus, although the important things
are splendidly achieved,
you cannot explain to anyone
how they got done.

That is what happens
when you rest in the Tao.
You do nothing and the universe works
like a well-ordered machine.

Rely on your own efforts
and you make a mess of things;
Rely on the Tao and you allow
the inherent perfection of life

to be simply
and profoundly expressed.

49

The wise one understands people
because she joins with them in their hearts.

She inspires goodness in those who are good
and in those who are not so good.

In this way, goodness becomes a virtue.

She inspires trust in those who are trustworthy
and in those who are not so trustworthy.

In this way, trust becomes a virtue.

Because she sees the essence of each person
and is impartial in her dealings with others,

people learn to see each other clearly
and to treat each other fairly.

Compassionate and inclusive,
she treats all people as her children.

50

Some people live afraid to die.
Others die afraid to live.
Only a few people live
without fearing life or death.

When they travel,
wild buffalo attack them
but can find no place to strike them
with their horns.

Wild tigers pounce on them
but can find no place
to pierce them
with their claws.

Serving in the army,
weapons are pointed at them
in the heat of battle,
but they are not wounded.

Not fearing death,
it does not stop them.
Not fearing life,
it does not pass them by.

51

Tao gives birth to us,
nurtures us, and sustains us.

She helps us learn to trust
our potential
and bring it to completion.

Honoring Tao is not difficult.
We do so naturally
by accepting ourselves and others.

Only when we try to follow or lead,
do we lose our connection
to the Source.

Tao guides us back to center
when we have moved
off-course.

She protects us from danger
without following us
or holding us back.

She keeps us from trespassing
without controlling
what we do or say.

That is why she has been called
"the mysterious virtue."

No matter how far we stray
from her nurturing embrace,

we remain only a heartbeat away
from her guidance and her grace.

52

Tao is the Mother of all things.

If you know the Mother,
you can know the child.

Yet when you know the child,
do not let go of the Mother.

That would be like holding onto the branches
and releasing the roots.

It would be the beginning of disaster.

Close the door to desire.
Don't waste your time out on a limb
seeking the fruit before it falls.

Close up the apertures. Return to the roots.

Most people seek external greatness,
but the Taoist is content
with the insignificant and the small.

Most people seek the hard and the shiny,
but the Taoist is content
with the soft and the dim.

Because his light is well hidden,
he walks unseen through the darkness.

Surrounded by danger,
he never experiences harm.

Battles may wage all around him
yet he rests secure in his Mother's arms.

53

Understanding the greatness of the Tao,
I do not question it.

My only fear is that I might meddle with it.

The way of Tao is smooth and straight.
Anyone who trusts it can follow it.

Yet how often do we trust it?

Some people think "there must be a shortcut!"
Others try to twist Tao to suit their goals.

Isn't it strange that the people's fields
are overgrown with weeds

and their granaries are empty
while our leaders live in great abundance?

Do you find it rather odd that they,
dressed in extravagant clothes,

their tables overflowing with food and drink
they cannot possibly consume,

would nonetheless have us believe
that they are following the path of Tao?

54

Plant the roots firmly in the ground
and the tree will grow strong
and not easily be uprooted.

Carry the vessel securely in your hands
and it will not slip
and fall to the ground.

Live a simple and virtuous life
and you will pass the wisdom of Tao
along to others.

Cultivating Tao in yourself,
you will be authentic
and whole.

Cultivating Tao in your family,
you will live together
in harmony.

Cultivating Tao in your village,
the inhabitants
will prosper.

Cultivating Tao in your country,
people with different beliefs
will be at peace.

How do I know this?
Because everything under heaven
has its roots in the same Tao.

55

One who has inner virtue
is like an infant.
He is not aggressive
toward any creature.

Wasps do not sting him.
Scorpions do not bite him.
Tigers do not claw him.
Birds of prey do not eat him.

His muscles may be soft,
but his grip is firm.
Although he is chaste,
his virility is not doubted.

Childlike and innocent,
his vital force and creativity
are completely contained
within his heart/mind.

While others cling to life
and die an early death,
he looks death in the eye,
and lives a lengthy life.

56

The one who knows does not speak.
The one who speaks does not know.

Eliminate desires and cravings.
Curb your intellect.
Cut out contention.

Go towards the light.
Merge with the dust.

When you join with the mystery,
people cannot find you
or escape you.

They cannot benefit you or harm you,
lift you up or pull you down.

Like water moving through a sieve,
only your essence remains,
free of entanglements.

57

If one tries to govern the people,
he will act too harshly.

Only one who tends to matters
without conscious purpose
acts with heaven on his side.

Why is this?

Because when the state
establishes rules and prohibitions,
people become unruly.

When force is used against them,
people resist.

More laws attract more criminals.
More criminals attract more laws.
It is a vicious cycle.

The more clever and calculating
the leader becomes,

the more his government
begins to fall apart.

Thus, the wise leader
engages in no conscious effort
and things fall into place.

He sits quietly and peacefully,
and people govern themselves.

He lives without riches,
and people realize they have enough.

He lives free of desires,
and people lead virtuous lives.

58

Wise leaders stay well hidden
and people live in a simple, trusting,
open-hearted manner.

Foolish leaders are conspicuous
and look too closely into people's affairs.

Thus, people become suspicious,
calculating, and devious.

What is the best government?
When order arises spontaneously
and there is no governing at all!

Can you correct without blaming
or redeem without shaming?

After so many years of meddling
by their leaders, people are confused.

That is why the wise one helps people
come back into alignment,
but he does not judge them.

He tells them the truth
but he does not offend them.

He helps people stand straight,
but doesn't mention the crooked things
they have done in the past.

He shines his light,
not to expose the weakness of others,
but to guide them into their strength.

59

The gardener understands
how to serve heaven.
She plants the seed in the earth,
waters it, and watches it
grow to maturity.

When weeds grow around it,
she pulls them out.

Tend your life in the same way.
Establish yourself
in your essence;
don't let cravings
and desires take root.

This simple practice
is the quickest way
to realization: in every moment,
cling to the roots
and pull out the weeds.

Nurture virtue in this way
and there is no limit
to what you can accomplish.
The state thrives
because the leader

tends to the roots first
and then turns to the branch tips.

60

Ruling the state is like cooking a small fish.
Stirring leads to disaster.

Being centered and quiet in himself,
the leader is not undermined

by his own desires
or thrown off track by the desires of others.

Because he joins with the Tao,
even the hungry ghosts cannot sway him.

In the end, they too revert to the Tao.

Light a small fire under the pan
and the fish cooks easily.

Do the absolute minimum
and even a large state runs itself.

61

The large state is like a great sea
into which all rivers flow.

This is the mysterious female.
Assuming the lowest position,
she arouses the male
and draws him toward her.

The wise leader knows that such humility
is a sign of strength.

He knows that when the strong
places itself under the weak,
the weak will surrender to it.
Isn't this better than using force?

Thus, a small state gains security
by merging into a larger state.
A large state grows in size
by absorbing smaller states.

By assuming the correct position,
both get what they want.

62

Tao is the shelter of all beings.

It is the treasure of the good person
and the protector
of the not so good person.

Even those who do not understand Tao
are nurtured by it.

Although it is priceless,
all things derive their value from it.

Although it is silent and still,
great words and noble deeds arise from it.

While the three dukes
could be given jade disks to hold
and teams of horses to lead the way,

this would express Tao less
than just letting them sit quietly.

Tao is beyond our capacity
to conceive or measure.

It rewards the virtuous person.
It forgives the angry one.

All beings return to it when it is time.

63

The wise one seems to act
without moving.

She seems to get things done
without laboring.

She treats small matters
as though they were great,

and a few people
as though they were many.

Knowing great things begin small
she reaches her goal

by taking many
small steps forward.

Not taking success for granted,
she remains alert.

Not underestimating difficulties,
she is not caught off guard.

Addressing problems early on,
she nips trouble in the bud.

Thus, without struggling,
she overcomes all obstacles.

Without trying to be great,
she fulfills her greatness.

64

Security is easy to maintain if you are alert.
Acting before disorder takes root
you keep order in the state.

Even conditions that take root
are easy to eradicate
when they are small and weak.

But what begins small and weak
grows to be large and strong.
What was moveable becomes immovable.

A tiny shoot becomes a towering tree.
A pile of dirt becomes a nine-story terrace.
A single step turns into a thousand mile journey.

If you don't uproot danger when it is small,
but try to control it when it is strong,
you will meet with disaster.

Because the wise one anticipates difficulties
and nips trouble in the bud,
he is spared taking futile actions in the future.

Not valuing luxuries or indulging desires,
he is not lured off the path
when his goal is in sight.

Indeed, he remains vigilant,
knowing that many suffer ruin
just when they are about to succeed.

Alert at the end as he was at the beginning,
he fulfills his purpose
and completes his journey.

Following his lead,
people simplify their lives
and focus on the task at hand.

65

The ancient Taoists
helped people revert
to their original natures.

They discouraged people
from gathering knowledge
or becoming clever.

They advised their leaders
not to use knowledge
to govern the state.

Trusting their intuition,
the great leaders
simplified their lives

and people began to fulfill
their potential
without envy or struggle.

Thus, the state prospered.
What was true then
is no less true today.

Governing without knowledge
is the consistent rule.
It is the mysterious virtue.

It helps leaders be authentic.
It helps people be true
to themselves.

66

Streams flow into the river below.
Seeking the lowest place,
rivers flow into the sea.

To win people's admiration,
serve them with humility.
To lead, follow them for a while.

Be light in your ways
and people will not experience
your guidance as heavy.

Be inconspicuous
and they won't view your presence
as an obstacle.

Don't contend with others,
and people will keep
nominating you.

Be peaceful and still,
and all of heaven will continue
singing your praises.

67

Everyone says that Tao is great,
but it has no image.
If Tao could be imagined,
it would not be great.

There are three treasures
that we value:
the first is compassion,
the second is frugality,
and the third, humility.

Thanks to compassion,
we can be brave.
Thanks to frugality,
we can be generous.
Thanks to humility,
we can lead others.

One who is brave,
but not compassionate,
will meet an early death.

One who is generous,
but has no means,
will end his life
begging on the street.

One who can lead,
but has no humility,
will know ignominy
and disgrace.

Only compassion,
frugality and humility
can protect us,
shelter us, and help us
win the victory.

68

The great general does not like war.
He is slow to anger
and keeps a safe distance from the enemy.
He places the good of his soldiers above his own.

Because he is careful and respectful of others,
virtue and power belong to him.
He is worthy of heaven.
Only a fool goes into battle against such a man.

69

The great general doesn't look
for trouble, but he is prepared
when trouble comes to him.
He would rather retreat a foot
than advance an inch.

Moving his troops around
with no apparent reason,
he pushes up his sleeve,
without exposing his arm.
His men are visible,
but their weapons can't be seen.

Few would challenge him,
yet he is ready for an opponent.
Without worthy opposition,
too much power goes to one side
and the three treasures are lost.

When a worthy opponent comes
and his army is evenly matched,
he goes into battle reluctantly,
showing mercy and restraint.
For this reason alone,
he emerges victorious.

70

My words are easy to understand and practice,
yet only a few understand or practice them.

My words and actions have an origin.
It is because this origin is not known
that few people understand me.

Wise men and women are rare.
They may look like others,
but their words and deeds are distinct.

They may wear coarse woolen clothes,
but the jewel of truth shines in their hearts.

71

Knowing can be helpful,
but not knowing is more helpful.

Better still is knowing that you don't know.

Those who know are skillful
and avoid the places where the forest burns.

Those who do not know are innocent
and guided by grace away from harm.

Those who know that they don't know
are both skillful and innocent.

They walk through the burning forest
without being touched by the flames.

72

When people are free to live
according to their nature,
they stay rooted in truth
and maintain peace by themselves.

When people are controlled
by soldiers and laws,
they lose touch with truth
and erupt in angry rebellion.

The wise leader knows
that people who are not trusted
become disturbed and confused.
Nothing satisfies them.

So he listens to people's concerns
and regains their trust.

When safety is reestablished,
people feel content once again.

Because he offers trust, he receives it.
While others want to use force,
he prefers to bring back order
with acceptance and love.

73

If one is brave, but not reckless,
he will live a full life.

If one is brave and also reckless,
he will die an early death.

There are exceptions to this rule,
but the wise one doesn't look for them.

She finds a way to win
without contending with others.

She finds a way to communicate
without speaking.

She finds a way to attract people
without calling to them.

Trusting the signs heaven sends,
she is ever at ease with what happens.

She knows that the net of heaven
is spread far and wide.

Although its mesh is coarse,
it never loses anything of value.

74

The great executioner puts people to death
without fail when their time comes.

Do you want to take over his job?

If the state decides who lives and who dies,
innocent people may be put to death.

Isn't this like trying to build a house
when you don't know how to cut straight?

A little mistake and you might lose a finger.

The master carpenter is standing nearby.
Why not leave the cutting to him?

75

The ruler's table overflows with food and drink
yet the people starve.

Why is this?
Because he taxes them unfairly.

The ruler criticizes the people
because they are discontent and unruly.

But I say it is the ruler's fault.

If he did not indulge his cravings,
they would not drink away the little they have.

If he did not live a life of arrogance and greed,
they would not steal from each other.

If he did not bear down so hard on them,
order and discipline would become

a natural part of their lives.

76

When they are alive,
people are soft and flexible.

When they are dead,
people are hard and stiff.

Soft and flexible
is the language of life.

Hard and stiff
is the language of death.

A tree that does not bend
is broken in the wind.

Its solidity is undermined
by termites.

When leaders act in ways
that are harsh and inflexible,

people refuse to help them
and plot to bring them down.

The strength of a true leader
lies in his humility.

He is steady and reliable
like the trunk of a tree.

When the people know
their leader supports them,

they are soft and pliant
like branches

dancing in the wind.
They sing out his praises.

They are happy to assist him
in any way that they can.

77

Tao works like the string of a bow.
As the archer pulls the string back,
the top of the bow is pulled down
and the bottom of the bow
is pulled up.

Tao naturally brings high and low
toward each other.
It naturally takes
from the rich
and gives to the poor.

Human laws function differently.
They accentuate the gap
between high and low.
They take from the poor
and give to the rich.

Paying more attention to the target
than to the archer,
people are surprised
when the bow string slackens
and the arrow falls to the ground.

The Taoist sees this coming,
but prefers to remain silent.
Although he is a master of archery,
he would rather be its student
than its teacher.

Although he knows the Tao,
he prefers to observe
its magnificent ways,
than to interfere in the masterly lessons
it teaches us.

78

Nothing under heaven
is softer and more pliant
than water,

yet nothing is as effective
for defeating
the hard and the stiff.

All of us know this,
but we don't remember
to practice it.

We meet force with force,
forgetting that the gentle
quietly overcomes

the harsh;
we take dogmatic positions,
forgetting that the flexible

eventually surrounds
and overcomes
the rigid.

Following the logic
of the past,
we continue to do

what has been done to us,
forgetting that truth,
being new,

is neither logical
nor familiar.
It asks us to respond

to old triggers
in a new way.

79

When one lets others go too far,
resentment is born.

That is why the sage looks within
for cause of trespass.

He does not blame others
for what he thinks and feels.

He looks at his own thoughts.
He scrutinizes his own actions.

He looks at his side of the tally
and throws the other side away.

He holds himself responsible.
He holds others harmless.

80

Let the state be small and the people few.

Let the military be no larger than a company.
Then, it would never be used.

Let the people be aware of the dangers of travel
and they would not go far.

Although they had boats and carriages,
they would not ride in them.

Content eating their own food,
wearing their own clothes,

and living in their own houses,
they would have no reason to leave their village.

Although they might have a distant view
of another town,

and hear the sound of dogs and chickens
echoing across the valley,

they would have no occasion to visit there.
Growing old in their own village,

undistracted by the outside world,
they would sink their roots

deeper and deeper
into the place of their origin.

81

Words that are true are not always beautiful.
Beautiful words are not always true.

The benevolent ones do not argue or fight.
Those who argue or fight are not benevolent.

Those who know the truth do not collect facts.
Those who collect facts don't know the truth.

The wise one seeks nothing for himself.
He gives away everything he has.

Since what he gives away returns to him,
he never lacks for resources.

He never stops giving.
He never stops serving.

He benefits others without doing harm.
He acts without stirring things up.

APPENDICES

List of Poems

PART 2 TAO te CHING

List of Illustrations

Portions have been used from the following paintings:

292

Paul Ferrini's unique blend of radical Christianity and other wisdom traditions, goes beyond self-help and recovery into the heart of healing. He is the author of twenty-four books including his latest books *Enlightenment for Everyone, I am the Door, Reflections of the Christ Mind* and *The Way of Peace.* His *Christ Mind* Series includes the bestseller *Love Without Conditions, The Silence of the Heart, Miracle of Love* and *Return to the Garden.* Other recent books include *Creating a Spiritual Relationship, Grace Unfolding, Living in the Heart, Crossing the Water, The Ecstatic Moment* and *Illuminations on the Road to Nowhere.*

Paul Ferrini is the founder and editor of *Miracles Magazine* and a nationally known teacher and workshop leader. His conferences, retreats, and *Affinity Group Process* have helped thousands of people deepen their practice of forgiveness and open their hearts to the divine presence in themselves and others. For more information on Paul's workshops and retreats or The *Affinity Group Process,* contact Heartways Press, P. O. Box 99, Greenfield, MA 01302-0099 or call 413-774-9474.

BOOKS AND TAPES
AVAILABLE FROM HEARTWAYS PRESS

Paul Ferrini's luminous new translation captures the essence of Lao Tzu and the fundamental aspects of Taoism in a way that no single book ever has!

The Great Way of All Beings:
Renderings of Lao Tzu
by Paul Ferrini
ISBN 1-879159-46-5
320 pages hardcover
$23.00

New

The Great Way of All Beings: Renderings of Lao Tzu is composed of two different versions of Lao Tzu's masterful scripture *Tao Te Ching*. Part one, River of Light, is an intuitive, spontaneous rendering of the material that captures the spirit of the *Tao Te Ching*, but does not presume to be a close translation. Part Two is a more conservative translation of the *Tao Te Ching* that attempts as much as possible to stay with the words and images used in the original text. The words and images used in Part One leap out from the center to explore how the wisdom of the Tao touches us today. By contrast, the words and images of Part Two turn inward toward the center, offering a more feminine, receptive version of the material.

> *"We listen for it, yet its note can't be heard.*
> *We look intently for it, yet its image can't be seen.*
>
> *Although it has no beginning,*
> *it leads us back to our original nature*
>
> *Although it has no end,*
> *it helps us come to completion."*

A Practical Guide to Realizing your True Nature

"Enlightenment is the realization of the light that is within you. It is the conscious recognition and acceptance of that light. Enlightenment is discovering who you already are and being it fully."

Enlightenment for Everyone
by Paul Ferrini
ISBN 1-879159-45-7
160 pages hardcover $16.00

Enlightenment is not contingent on finding the right teacher or having some kind of peak spiritual experience. There's nothing that you need to get, find or acquire to be enlightened. You don't need a priest or rabbi to intercede with God for you. You don't need a special technique or meditation practice. You don't need to memorize scripture or engage in esoteric breathing practices. You simply need to discover who you already are and be it fully. This essential guide to self-realization contains eighteen spiritual practices that will enable you to awaken to the truth of your being. This exquisite hard-cover book will be a life-long companion and will make an inspirational gift to friends and family.

*A comprehensive selection from the Christ Mind
teachings just released by Doubleday*

"*Open yourself now to the wisdom of Jesus, as Paul Ferrini has
brought it through. These words can inspire you to greater
insights and understandings, to more clarity and a grander resolve
to make changes in your life that can truly change the world.*"

Neale Donald Walsch, author of Conversations with God.

Reflections of the Christ Mind:
The Present Day
Teachings of Jesus
by Paul Ferrini
Introduction by Neale Donald
Walsch
ISBN 0-385-49952-3
302 pages hardcover $19.95

Reflections of the Christ Mind contains
key excerpts from *Love Without Conditions, Silence of the
Heart, Miracle of Love* and *Return to the Garden*. It presents
the most important teachings in the *Christ Mind* series.

I am the Door
by Paul Ferrini
ISBN 1-879159-41-4
288 pages hardcover $21.95

Years ago, Paul Ferrini began hearing a persistent inner voice that said "I want you to acknowledge me." He also had a series of dreams in which Jesus appeared to teach him. Later, when Ferrini's relationship with his teacher was firmly established, the four books in the *Reflections of the Christ Mind* series were published. Here, in this lovely lyrical collection, we can hear the voice of Jesus speaking directly to us about practical topics of everyday life that are close to our hearts like work and livelihood, relationships, community, forgiveness, spiritual practices, and miracles. When you put this book down, there will no doubt in your mind that the teachings of the master are alive today. Your life will never be the same.

Taking Back Our Schools
by Paul Ferrini
ISBN 1-879159-43-0
$10.95

This book is written for parents who are concerned about the education of their children. It presents a simple idea that could transform the school system in this country. This book does not pretend to have all the answers. It is the start of a conversation. It is chapter one in a larger book that has not yet been written. If you choose to work with these ideas, you may be one of the authors of the chapters to come.

The Way of Peace
by Paul Ferrini
ISBN 1-879159-42-2
256 pages hardcover
$19.95

The Way of Peace is a simple method for connecting with the wisdom and truth that lie within our hearts. The two hundred and sixteen oracular messages in this book were culled from the bestselling *Reflections of the Christ Mind* series by Paul Ferrini.

Open this little book spontaneously to receive inspirational guidance, or ask a formal question and follow the simple divinatory procedure described in the introduction. You will be amazed at the depth and the accuracy of the response you receive.

Like the *I-Ching,* the *Book of Runes,* and other systems of guidance, *The Way of Peace* empowers you to connect with peace within and act in harmony with your true self and the unique circumstances of your life.

Special dice, blessed by the author, are available for using *The Way of Peace* as an oracle. To order these dice, send $3.00 plus shipping.

"The Road to Nowhere *is the path through your heart. It is not a journey of escape. It is a journey through your pain to end the pain of separation."*

Illuminations on the Road to Nowhere
160 pages paperback $12.95
ISBN 1-879159-44-9

There comes a time for all of us when the outer destinations no longer satisfy and we finally understand that the love and happiness we seek cannot be found out-side of us. It must be found in our own hearts, on the other side of our pain.

This book makes it clear that we can no longer rely on outer teachers or teachings to find our spiritual identity. Nor can we find who we are in relationships where boundaries are blurred and one person makes decisions for another. If we want to be authentic, we can't allow anyone else to be an authority for us, nor can we allow ourselves to be an authority for another person.

This provocative book challenges many of our basic assumptions about personal happiness and the meaning of our relationship with others and with God.

Our Surrender Invites Grace

Grace Unfolding: The Art of Living A Surrendered Life
96 pages paperback $9.95
ISBN 1-879159-37-6

As we surrender to the truth of our being, we learn to relinquish the need to control our lives, figure things out, or predict the future. We begin to let go of our judgments and interpretations and accept life the way it is. When we can be fully present with whatever life brings, we are guided to take the next step on our journey. That is the way that grace unfolds in our lives.

The Relationship Book You've Been Waiting For

Creating a Spiritual Relationship: A Guide to Growth and Happiness for Couples on the Path
144 pages paperback $10.95
ISBN 1-879159-39-2

This simple but profound guide to growth and happiness for couples will help you and your partner:

- Make a realistic commitment to each other
- Develop a shared experience that nurtures your relationship
- Give each other the space to grow and express yourselves as individuals
- Communicate by listening without judgment and telling the truth in a non-blaming way
- Understand how you mirror each other
- Stop blaming your partner and take responsibility for your thoughts, feelings and actions
- Practice forgiveness together on an ongoing basis

These seven spiritual principles will help you weather the ups and downs of your relationship so that you and your partner can grow together and deepen the intimacy between you. The book also includes a special section on living alone and preparing to be in relationship and a section on separating with love when a relationship needs to change form or come to completion.

Return to the Garden
Reflections of The Christ Mind,
Part IV
$12.95, Paperback
ISBN 1-879159-35-X

"In the Garden, all our needs were provided for. We knew no struggle or hardship. We were God's beloved. But happiness was not enough for us. We wanted the freedom to live our own lives. To evolve, we had to learn to become love-givers, not just love-receivers.

We all know what happened then. We were cast out of the Garden and for the first time in our lives we felt shame, jealousy, anger, lack. We experienced highs and lows, joy and sorrow. Our lives became difficult. We had to work hard to survive. We had to make mistakes and learn from them. Initially, we tried to blame others for our mistakes. But that did not make our lives any easier. It just deepened our pain and misery. We had to learn to face our fears, instead of projecting them onto each other.

Returning to the Garden, we are different than we were when we left hellbent on expressing our creativity at any cost. We return humble and sensitive to the needs of all. We return not just as created, but as co-creator, not just as son of man, but also as son of God."

Learn the Spiritual Practice
Associated with the Christ Mind Teachings

Living in the Heart The Affinity
Process and the Path of
Unconditional Love and Acceptance
Paperback $10.95
ISBN 1-879159-36-8

The long awaited, definitive book on the
Affinity Process is finally here. For years, the
Affinity Process has been refined by participants so that it
could be easily understood and experienced. Now, you
can learn how to hold a safe, loving, non-judgmental space
for yourself and others which will enable you to open
your heart and move through your fears. The *Affinity
Process* will help you learn to take responsibility for your
fears and judgments so that you won't project them onto
others. It will help you learn to listen deeply and without
judgment to others. And it will teach you how to tell your
truth clearly without blaming others for your experience.
Part One contains an in-depth description of the principles
on which the *Affinity Process* is based. Part Two contains a
detailed discussion of the *Affinity Group Guidelines*. And Part
Three contains a manual for people who wish to facilitate
an *Affinity Group* in their community.

If you are a serious student of the *Christ Mind* teachings,
this book is essential for you. It will enable you to begin a
spiritual practice which will transform your life and the lives
of others. It will also offer you a way of extending the teachings of love and forgiveness throughout your community.

Now Finally our Bestselling Title on Audio Tape

Love Without Conditions,
Reflections of the Christ Mind, Part I

by Paul Ferrini
The Book on Tape Read by the Author
2 Cassettes, Approximately 3.25 hours
ISBN 1-879159-24-4 $19.95

Now on audio tape: the incredible book from Jesus calling us to awaken to our own Christhood. Listen to this gentle, profound book while driving in your car or before going to sleep at night. Elisabeth Kubler-Ross calls this "the most important book I have read. I study it like a Bible." Find out for yourself how this amazing book has helped thousands of people understand the radical teachings of Jesus and begin to integrate these teachings into their lives.

With its heartfelt combination of sensuality and spirituality, Paul Ferrini's poetry has been compared to the poetry of Rumi.

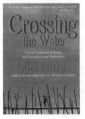

Crossing The Water:
Poems About Healing
and Forgiveness in
Our Relationships

The time for healing and reconciliation has come, Ferrini writes. Our relationships help us heal childhood wounds, walk through our deepest fears, and cross over the water of our emotional pain. Just as the rocks in the river are pounded and caressed to rounded stone, the rough edges of our personalities are worn smooth in the context of a committed relationship. If we can keep our hearts open, we can heal together, experience genuine equality, and discover what it means to give and receive love without conditions.

With its heartfelt combination of sensuality and spirituality, Paul Ferrini's poetry has been compared to the poetry of Rumi. These luminous poems demonstrate why Paul Ferrini is first a poet, a lover and a mystic. Come to this feast of the beloved with an open heart and open ears. 96 pp. paper ISBN 1-879159-25-2 $9.95.

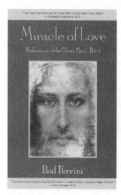

Miracle of Love: Reflections of the Christ Mind, Part III

In this volume of the Christ Mind series, Jesus sets the record straight regarding a number of events in his life. He tells us: "I was born to a simple woman in a barn. She was no more a virgin than your mother was." Moreover, the virgin birth was not the only myth surrounding his life and teaching. So were the concepts of vicarious atonement and physical resurrection.

Relentlessly, the master tears down the rigid dogma and hierarchical teachings that obscure his simple message of love and forgiveness. He encourages us to take him down from the pedestal and the cross and see him as an equal brother who found the way out of suffering by opening his heart totally. We too can open our hearts and find peace and happiness. "The power of love will make miracles in your life as wonderful as any attributed to me," he tells us. "Your birth into this embodiment is no less holy than mine. The love that you extend to others is no less important than the love I extend to you." 192 pp. paper ISBN 1-879159-23-6 $12.95.

The Ecstatic Moment: A Practical Manual for Opening Your Heart and Staying in It.

A simple, power-packed guide that helps us take appropriate responsibility for our experience and establish healthy boundaries with others. Part II contains many helpful exercises and meditations that teach us to stay centered, clear and open in heart and mind. The *Affinity Group Process* and other group practices help us learn important listening and communication skills that can transform our troubled relationships. Once you have read this book, you will keep it in your briefcase or on your bedside table, referring to it often. You will not find a more practical, down to earth guide to contemporary spirituality. You will want to order copies for all your friends. 128 pp. paper ISBN 1-879159-18-X $10.95

The Silence of the Heart: Reflections of the Christ Mind, Part II

A powerful sequel to *Love Without Conditions.* John Bradshaw says: "with deep insight and sparkling clarity, this book demonstrates that the roots of all abuse are to be found in our own self-betrayal. Paul Ferrini leads us skillfully and courageously beyond shame, blame, and attachment to our wounds into the depths of self-forgiveness...a must read for all people who are ready to take responsibility for their own healing." 218 pp. paper. ISBN 1-879159-16-3 $14.95

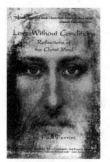

Love Without Conditions: Reflections of the Christ Mind, Part I

An incredible book calling us to awaken to our Christhood. Rarely has any book conveyed the teachings of the master in such a simple but profound manner. This book will help you to bring your understanding from the head to the heart so that you can model the teachings of love and forgiveness in your daily life. 192 pp. paper ISBN 1-879159-15-5 $12.00

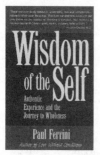

The Wisdom of the Self

This ground-breaking book explores our authentic experience and our journey to wholeness. "Your life is your spiritual path. Don't be quick to abandon it for promises of bigger and better experiences. You are getting exactly the experiences you need to grow. If your growth seems too slow or uneventful for you, it is because you have not fully embraced the situations and relationships at hand...To know the Self is to allow everything, to embrace the totality of who we are, all that we think and feel, all of our fear, all of our love." 229 pp. paper ISBN 1-879159-14-7 $12.00

The Twelve Steps of Forgiveness

A practical manual for healing ourselves and our relationships. This book gives us a step-by-step process for moving through our fears, projections, judgments, and guilt so that we can take responsibility for creating the life we want. With great gentleness, we learn to embrace our lessons and to find equality with others. 128 pp. paper ISBN 1-879159-10-4 $10.00

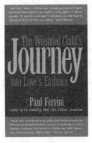

The Wounded Child's Journey: Into Love's Embrace

This book explores a healing process in which we confront our deep-seated guilt and fear, bringing love and forgiveness to the wounded child within. By surrendering our judgments of self and others, we overcome feelings of separation and dismantle co-dependent patterns that restrict our self-expression and ability to give and receive love. 225pp. paper ISBN 1-879159-06-6 $12.00

The Bridge to Reality

A Heart-Centered Approach to *A Course in Miracles* and the Process of Inner Healing. Sharing his experiences of spiritual awakening, Paul emphasizes self-acceptance and forgiveness as cornerstones of spiritual practice. Presented with beautiful photos, this book conveys the essence of The Course as it is lived in daily life. 192 pp. paper ISBN 1-879159-03-1 $12.00

Virtues of The Way

A lyrical work of contemporary scripture reminiscent of the *Tao Te Ching*. Beautifully illustrated, this inspirational book will help you cultivate the spiritual values required to fulfill your creative purpose and live in harmony with others. 64 pp. paper ISBN 1-879159-02-3 $7.50

From Ego to Self

108 illustrated affirmations designed to offer you a new way of viewing conflict situations so that you can overcome negative thinking and bring more energy, faith and optimism into your life. 144 pp. paper ISBN 1-879159-01-5 $10.00

The Body of Truth

A crystal clear introduction to the universal teachings of love and forgiveness. This book traces all forms of suffering to negative attitudes and false beliefs, which we have the ability to transform. 64 pp. paper ISBN 1-879159-02-3 $7.50

Available Light

Inspirational, passionate poems dealing with the work of inner integration, love and relationships, death and re-birth, loss and abundance, life purpose and the reality of spiritual vision. 128 pp. paper ISBN 1-879159-05-8 $12.00

Poetry and Guided Meditation Tapes
by Paul Ferrini

The Poetry of the Soul

With its heartfelt combination of sensuality and spirituality, Paul Ferrini's poetry has been compared to the poetry of Rumi. These luminous poems read by the author demonstrate why Paul Ferrini is first a poet, a lover and a mystic. Come to this feast of the beloved with an open heart and open ears. With Suzi Kesler on piano. $10.00 ISBN 1-879159-26-0

The Circle of Healing

The meditation and healing tape that many of you have been seeking. This gentle meditation opens the heart to love's presence and extends that love to all the beings in your experience. A powerful tape with inspirational piano accompaniment by Michael Gray. ISBN 1-879159-08-2 $10.00

Healing the Wounded Child

A potent healing tape that accesses old feelings of pain, fragmentation, self-judgment and separation and brings them into the light of conscious awareness and acceptance. Side two includes a hauntingly beautiful "inner child" reading from The Bridge to Reality with piano accompaniment by Michael Gray. ISBN 1-879159-11-2 $10.00

Forgiveness: Returning to the Original Blessing

A self healing tape that helps us accept and learn from the mistakes we have made in the past. By letting go of our judgments and ending our ego-based search for perfection, we can bring our darkness to the light, dissolving anger, guilt, and shame. Piano accompaniment by Michael Gray. ISBN 1-879159-12-0 $10.00

Paul Ferrini Talks and Workshop Tapes

Answering Our Own Call for Love

Paul tells the story of his own spiritual awakening: his Atheist upbringing, how he began to open to the presence of God, and his connection with Jesus and the Christ Mind teaching. In a very clear, heart-felt way, Paul presents to us the spiritual path of love, acceptance, and forgiveness. 1 Cassette $10.00 ISBN 1-879159-33-3

The Ecstatic Moment

Shows us how we can be with our pain compassionately and learn to nurture the light within ourselves, even when it appears that we are walking through darkness. Discusses subjects such as living in the present, acceptance, not fixing self or others, being with our discomfort and learning that we are lovable as we are. 1 Cassette $10.00 ISBN 1-879159-27-9

Honoring Self and Other

Helps us understand the importance of not betraying ourselves in our relationships with others. Focuses on understanding healthy boundaries, setting limits, and saying no to others in a loving way. Real life examples include a woman who is married to a man who is chronically critical of her, and a gay man who wants to tell his judgmental parents that he has AIDS. 1 Cassette $10.00 ISBN 1-879159-34-1

Seek First the Kingdom

Discusses the words of Jesus in the Sermon on the Mount: "Seek first the kingdom and all else will be added to you." Helps us understand how we create the inner temple by learning to hold our judgments of self and other more compassionately. The love of God flows through our love and acceptance of ourselves. As we establish our connection to the divine within ourselves, we don't need to look outside of ourselves for love and acceptance. Includes fabulous music by The Agape Choir and Band. 1 Cassette $10.00 ISBN 1-879159-30-9

Double Cassette Tape Sets

Ending the Betrayal of the Self

A roadmap for integrating the opposing voices in our psyche so that we can experience our own wholeness. Delineates what our responsibility is and isn't in our relationships with others, and helps us learn to set clear, firm, but loving boundaries. Our relationships can become areas of sharing and fulfillment, rather than mutual invitations to co-dependency and self betrayal. 2 Cassettes $16.95 ISBN 1-879159-28-7

Relationships: Changing Past Patterns

Begins with a Christ Mind talk describing the link between learning to love and accept ourselves and learning to love and accept others. Helps us understand how we are invested in the past and continue to replay our old relationship stories. Helps us get clear on what we want and understand how to be faithful to it. By being totally committed to ourselves, we give birth to the beloved within and also without. Includes an in-depth discussion about meditation, awareness, hearing our inner voice, and the Affinity Group Process. 2 Cassettes $16.95 ISBN 1-879159-32-5

Relationship As a Spiritual Path

Explores concrete ways in which we can develop a relationship with ourselves and learn to take responsibility for our own experience, instead of blaming others for our perceived unworthiness. Also discussed: accepting our differences, the new paradigm of relationship, the myth of the perfect partner, telling our truth, compassion vs. rescuing, the unavailable partner, abandonment issues, negotiating needs, when to say no, when to stay and work on a relationship and when to leave. 2 Cassettes $16.95 ISBN 1-879159-29-5

Opening to Christ Consciousness

Begins with a Christ Mind talk giving us a clear picture of how the divine spark dwells within each of us and how we can open up to God-consciousness on a regular basis. Deals with letting go and forgiveness in our relationships with our parents, our children and our partners. A joyful, funny, and scintillating tape you will want to listen to many times. 2 Cassettes $16.95 ISBN 1-879159-31-7

Poster and Notecards

Risen Christ Posters & Notecards
11" x 17"
Poster suitable for framing
ISBN 1-879159-19-8 $10.00

Set of 8 Notecards with Envelopes
ISBN 1-879159-20-1 $10.00

Ecstatic Moment Posters & Notecards

8.5" x 11"
Poster suitable for framing
ISBN 1-879159-21-X $5.00

Set of 8 Notecards with Envelopes
ISBN 1-879159-22-8 $10.00

Heartways Press Order Form

Name _____

Address _____

City _____State _____Zip _____

Phone/Fax_____Email _____

Books by Paul Ferrini

The Great Way of All Beings:
    Renderings of Lao Tzu Hardcover ($23.00) _____

Enlightenment for Everyone Hardcover ($16.00) _____

Taking Back Our Schools ($10.95) _____

The Way of Peace Hardcover ($19.95) _____

    Way of Peace Dice ($3.00) _____

Illuminations on the Road to Nowhere ($12.95) _____

I am the Door Hardcover ($21.95) _____

Reflections of the Christ Mind: The Present Day
    Teachings of Jesus Hardcover ($19.95) _____

Creating a Spiritual Relationship ($10.95) _____

Grace Unfolding: The Art of Living A
    Surrendered Life ($9.95) _____

Return to the Garden ($12.95) _____

Living in the Heart ($10.95) _____

Miracle of Love ($12.95) _____

Crossing the Water ($9.95) _____

The Ecstatic Moment ($10.95) _____

The Silence of the Heart ($14.95) _____

Love Without Conditions ($12.00) _____

The Wisdom of the Self ($12.00) _____

The Twelve Steps of Forgiveness ($10.00) _____

The Circle of Atonement ($12.00) _____

The Bridge to Reality ($12.00) _____

From Ego to Self ($10.00) _____

Virtues of the Way ($7.50) _____

The Body of Truth ($7.50) _____

Available Light ($10.00) _____

Audio Tapes by Paul Ferrini

The Circle of Healing ($10.00)   _____
Healing the Wounded Child ($10.00)   _____
Forgiveness: The Original Blessing ($10.00)   _____
The Poetry of the Soul ($10.00)   _____
Seek First the Kingdom ($10.00)   _____
Answering Our Own Call for Love ($10.00)   _____
The Ecstatic Moment ($10.00)   _____
Honoring Self and Other ($10.00)   _____
Love Without Conditions ($19.95) 2 tapes   _____
Ending the Betrayal of the Self ($16.95) 2 tapes   _____
Relationships: Changing Past Patterns ($16.95) 2 tapes   _____
Relationship As a Spiritual Path ($16.95) 2 tapes   _____
Opening to Christ Consciousness ($16.95) 2 tapes   _____

Posters and Notecards

Risen Christ Poster 11"x17" ($10.00)   _____
Ecstatic Moment Poster 8.5"x11" ($5.00)   _____
Risen Christ Notecards 8/pkg ($10.00)   _____
Ecstatic Moment Notecards 8/pkg ($10.00)   _____

Shipping

($2.50 for first item, $1.00 each additional item.   _____
Add additional $1.00 for first class postage   _____
and an extra $1.00 for hardcover books.)   _____
MA residents please add 5% sales tax.   _____
Please allow 1-2 weeks for delivery   TOTAL   _____

Send Order To: Heartways Press P. O. Box 99,
Greenfield, MA 01302-0099   413-774-9474
Toll free: 1-888-HARTWAY (Orders only)